knit with me

a mother & daughter collection

by Gudrun Johnston

with Quince & Co.

table of contents

I have a teenage daughter.

Maybe you do, too. Or you have a teen who's close to you in some way. If so, then you understand how frightening that can be. So many things to worry about, so many ways she's stepping into a world outside of the close years you've spent together.

However, there is so much that I love about seeing my daughter become a young woman. I'm incredibly proud of the person she's becoming, full of compassion and art and creativity. I wouldn't want Maya to be anyone other than who she is.

Fortunately, there are lots of ways that we're as close as ever. There are ways, even, that I inspire her, ways that she's proud of me! Chief among them is that she loves to wear designs I've knitted for her. In a time when peer pressure wants to push her toward a generic, commercially produced identity, she's found an appreciation for being unique. She's got knitwear created specifically for her, with designs that make her stand out. Even she'd admit it; her friends are jealous! Oh, the joy...

Not only does Maya want to wear my garments, she also wants to have a hand in creating them herself. Last winter, in Scotland, she knitted her first top-down sweater. She opted for a short-sleeved version to ease the process, and I may have worked a few rounds of the body for her, but the point is, she knitted her very first garment. For moral support, I worked the same sweater alongside her. We then had a fun little mother and daughter photo shoot in our new creations. This sparked an idea for a knitwear collection. *Knit With Me* was born.

Around the same time Pam Allen, of Quince & Co, approached me about the possibility of collaboration. It's no secret that I adore Quince yarns and have used them often, so saying yes wasn't very difficult! I already had a design in Quince's Chickadee yarn, my Soay cardigan. I had even knitted one for Maya in a different color. I decided that this design should be part of the collection and used it as a launching point for the rest of the sweater pairs in this book.

As I began to plan the collection, I thought of other friends with daughters of a similar age, all women who had unique relationships with their girls and who would be game for modeling. With Maya's input, I came up with designs inspired by these beautiful women (and young women). Maya drew me some sketches and we ended up with six pairs of sweaters that I believe work for mother and daughter alike. Ageless, you might say. The clean lines and simple details of these designs make them very versatile. They can be styled in a variety of ways to suit the age of the wearer! These sweater pairs form the first section of the book.

Initially, the vision for the collection was just about garments that could be worn by a mother and daughter. When considering what accessories to include, I thought it a good idea to include some patterns that would be accessible to newer knitters—patterns that a teen or anyone recently introduced to knitting could easily attempt. So I kept the accessory patterns simple, interesting to knit, with easy-to-work stitch patterns. Many of them are worked in Quince's Puffin, a chunky, quick-to-knit-up yarn!

Then I thought, why stop at simple accessories! What about a first sweater pattern? One of the first sweaters I ever knitted without a pattern was a top-down raglan with yarnover increases and little bell sleeves. That's what I re-created for the beginner sweater. Navigating patterns can be one of the most overwhelming aspects of knitting. So I wrote the pattern for the beginner sweater with lots of tips and detailed explanations to help guide the newer knitter through all the terminology.

It was so much fun to put this all together and to have my daughter be such an integral part of it, from the initial wearing of the knitwear to helping with the styling to providing illustrations for the book. This project belongs to her as much as to me.

I hope that *Knit With Me* has something for everyone. Perhaps your daughter, niece, sister, or mother will spot something she'd like you to knit for her, or maybe you can encourage her to try a simple accessory – or even to knit something for you!

Gudrun

the sweaters

Braeburn

Soay

McIntosh

Brock

Empire

Braeburn

This sweater is worked top down starting with the cowl. Stitches are picked up from the bound off edge of the cowl and the yoke is worked as a raglan to the underarms. The body has a gentle A-line shape with short rows worked at the bottom back hem making the back slightly longer than the front.

Finished measurements

31 ¾ (34 ¼, 36 ½, 39 ¾, 43 ¼, 46, 49 ½, 52 ¼, 55 ¾)" [80.5 (87.5, 92.5, 101, 110, 117, 125.5, 132.5, 141.5) cm] bust circumference
Shown in 34 ¼" [87.5 cm] with 6.25" positive ease, and 36 ½" [92.5 cm] with ½" negative ease.

Yarn

Lark by Quince & Co.
(100% American wool; 134 yd [123 m] / 50 g)
• 9 (10, 10, 11, 12, 13, 14, 15, 16) skeins in Iceland 153 or River 107
   Or 1155 (1250, 1325, 1450, 1570, 1670, 1800, 1900, 2025) yd worsted weight yarn.

Needles

• One 16", 24", and 32" circular needle (circ) in size US 8 [4 mm]
• One set of double-pointed needles (dpns) in size US 8 [4 mm] or one 40" circ if using magic loop to work sleeves

Or size to obtain gauge

Notions

• Stitch markers (m)
• Waste yarn
• Tapestry needle for weaving in ends
• Cable needle (optional)
• Two 4" strips of a contrasting color yarn in a similar weight to working yarn

Gauge

18 sts and 26 rnds = 4" [10 cm] in stockinette st, after blocking.
22 sts and 26 rnds = 4" [10 cm] in cable pattern, after blocking.
The center cable panel should measure approx 7" across at gauge after blocking.

Cable panel (total of 37 sts)

The crossed stitches in this pattern are formed without a cable needle. To ensure that the dropped sts don't unravel, keep movement of needles to a minimum when forming these sts. You can of course use a cable needle to hold the dropped sts if you prefer.

Right Twist: Sl 2 wyib, drop next st to front of work, slip same 2 sts back to LH needle, pick up dropped st and knit it, k2.
Left Twist: Drop next st to front of work, k2, pick up dropped st and knit it.

Rnd 1: P2, k3, p2, (k5, p4) twice, k5, p2, k3, p2.
Rnds 2–3: P2, k2, sl 1, p2, sl 1, k4, (p4, sl 1, k4) twice, p2, sl 1, k2, p2.
Rnd 4: P2, work a Right Twist (see instructions above), p2, work a Left Twist (see instructions above), k2, (p4, work a Left Twist, k2) twice, p2, work a Left Twist, p2.
Rnd 5: Repeat Rnd 1.
Rnds 6–7: P2, k2, sl 1, p2, (k4, sl 1, p4) twice, k4, sl 1, p2, sl 1, k2, p2.
Rnd 8: P2, work a Right Twist, p2, (k2, work a Right Twist, p4) twice, k2, work a Right Twist, p2, work a Left Twist, p2.
Repeat Rnds 1–8 for cable panel.

Pullover
Begin at cowl
Using medium circ and the long-tail cast on, CO 128 (128, 128, 136, 136, 136, 144, 144, 144) sts. Place marker (pm) for beg of rnd (BOR) and join for working in the rnd, being careful not to twist sts.
Rnd 1: *K2, p2; rep from * around.
Repeat Rnd 1 three times more.
Continue in St st in the rnd and work until cowl measures approx 9 ½" [24 cm] from CO edge.
Change to shorter circ. Next, follow directions for your size then, proceed to section marked All sizes resume.

Sizes 31 ¾, 34 ¼, 36 ½" [80.5 (87.5, 92.5) cm] only:
Next rnd *dec rnd:* K1, *k2, k2tog, k3, k2tog; rep from * to last st, k1 (28 sts dec'd)—100 sts remain.

Sizes 39 ¾, 43 ¼, 46" [101, 110, 117) cm] only:
Next rnd *dec rnd:* K2, *k3, k2tog, k4, k2tog; rep from * to last 2 sts, k2 (24 sts dec'd)—112 sts remain.

Sizes 49 ½, 52 ¼, 55 ¾" [125.5, 132.5, 141.5) cm] only:
Next rnd *dec rnd:* *K4, k2tog; rep from * around (24 sts dec'd)—120 sts remain.

All sizes resume:
BO all sts.

Begin yoke
Using shorter circ, pick up and knit 100 (100, 100, 112, 112, 112, 120, 120, 120) sts from BO edge of cowl.

Note: On next rnd, you will place a total of 7 markers—4 raglan seam markers, 2 markers to delineate cable panel, and 1 BOR marker. It may be a good idea to color co-ordinate the raglan seam markers so they are distinctive from the rest.

As you work the next rnd, you will begin the cable panel on the front. Use either the chart or written instructions and repeat Rnds 1–8 throughout body.

Set up rnd: Pm for BOR, k20 (20, 20, 22, 22, 22, 24, 24, 24), pm (raglan seam marker), k9 (9, 9, 11, 11, 11, 11, 11, 11), pm (raglan seam marker), k2 (2, 2, 4, 4, 4, 6, 6, 6), pm (for beg of cable panel), work Rnd 1 of cable panel over next 37 sts, pm (for end of cable panel), k2 (2, 2, 4, 4, 4, 6, 6, 6), pm (raglan seam marker), k9 (9, 9, 11, 11, 11, 11, 11, 11), pm (raglan seam marker), k21 (21, 21, 23, 23, 23, 25, 25, 25)—41 (41, 41, 45, 45, 45, 49, 49, 49) sts each for front and back; 9 (9, 9, 11, 11, 11, 11, 11, 11) sts each for sleeve.

Rnd 1 *inc rnd:* *Knit to 2 sts before raglan marker, k1-r/b, k1, sl m, k1, k1-r/b; rep from * once more, knit to first cable m, sl m, work next rnd of cable panel, ** knit to 2 st before raglan marker, k1-r/b, k1, sl m, k1, k1-r/b; rep from ** once more, knit to end (8 sts inc'd, one at either side of raglan marker points).
Rnd 2: Knit all sts and work requisite rnd of cable panel over the marked out cable panel sts.

Repeat Rnds 1 and 2 another 8 (11, 13, 11, 15, 17, 19, 21, 24) times, changing to longer circ as necessary—172 (196, 212, 208, 240, 256, 280, 296, 320) sts.

Next, follow directions for your size, then proceed to section marked All sizes resume.

Sizes 31 ¾ (34 ¼, 36 ½, 39 ¾)" [80.5 (87.5, 92.5, 101) cm] only:
Continue to increase on sleeve sts every other rnd 6 (6, 2, 2) times then every 4th rnd 0 (0, 3, 6) times **AND AT THE SAME TIME** increase on body sts every 4th rnd 3 (3, 4, 7) times—208 (232, 248, 268) sts total: 65 (71, 77, 83) sts each for front and back, and 39 (45, 47, 51) sts each for sleeve.
Work even in patt without increasing for 5 (5, 3, 1) more rnds.

Sizes 43 ¼, 46, 49 ½" [110, 117, 125.5) cm] only:
Repeat *inc rnd* every 4th rnd 6 (7, 7) times—288 (312, 336) sts total: 89 (95, 103) sts each for front and back; 55 (61, 65) sts each for sleeves.
Work even in patt without increasing for 1 (1, 1) rnd.

Sizes 52 ¼, 55 ¾" [132.5, 141.5 cm] only:
Repeat *inc rnd* every 4th rnd 6 (4) times, then continue to increase on body sts only every 4th rnd another 2 (4) times—352 (352) sts total: 109 (115) sts each for front and back; 67 (69) sts each for sleeves.

All sizes resume:
Divide for body and sleeves
(Remove raglan markers as you work the next rnd.)
Next rnd: *Knit to marker, place next 39 (45, 47, 51, 55, 61, 65, 67, 69) sts on waste yarn for sleeves, using the backward loop cast on, CO 4 (4, 4, 4, 5, 5, 5, 5, 6) sts, pm (side seam), CO 4 (4, 4, 4, 5, 5, 5, 5, 6) more sts; rep from * once more, working cable panel as normal, knit to end. Keep BOR marker in place—146 (158, 170, 182, 198, 210, 226, 238, 254) sts for body.

Work even in pattern for 15 (13, 15, 13, 13, 13, 13, 13, 15) rnds more, continuing to work the cabel panel as est.
Next rnd *inc rnd*: Knit to 2 sts before side seam marker, k1-r/b, k1, sl m, k1, k1-r/b; rep from * one time more (4 sts inc'd).

Continue in pattern as est and repeat *inc rnd* every 20th rnd 3 times more—162 (174, 186, 198, 214, 226, 242, 254, 270) sts total.
Work even in pattern without increasing for another 10 rnds. End having just worked Rnd 3 or 7 of cable panel.

Short rows to shape back
Note: You will be working back and forth across BOR marker as you work the short row section.
Short Row 1: Knit to 4 sts before side marker, turn work, place a strip of contrast color (CC) yarn across working yarn as for a Sunday Short Row (see techniques).
Short Row 2: Purl to 4 sts before other side seam marker, turn work, place a strip of CC yarn across working yarn as for a Sunday Short Row (see techniques).
Short Row 3: Knit to turning point (where CC yarn was placed), resolve short row for a RS row (see techniques), k3, turn work, place a strip of CC yarn across working yarn as for a Sunday Short Row.

Short Row 4: Purl to turning point (where CC yarn was placed), resolve short row for a WS row (see techniques), p3, turn work, place a strip of CC yarn across working yarn as for a Sunday Short Row.
Short Rows 5–6: Repeat Short Rows 3–4.
Short Row 7: Knit to turning point, resolve short row, k5, turn work, place a strip of CC yarn across working yarn.
Short Row 8: Purl to turning point, resolve short row, p5, turn work, place a strip of CC yarn across working yarn and knit back to beginning of rnd.

Next rnd: K1, work rest of rnd as normal, resolving final short rows as you come to them to 2 sts before end of rnd, k1-r/b, k1 (1 st inc'd)—163 (175, 187, 199, 215, 227, 243, 255, 271) sts total.
Next rnd: (P2, k2) to beginning of cable panel, work across cable panel as normal, (k2, p2) to last 2 sts, k2.
Repeat this last rnd for 7 rnds more. End after having worked Rnd 4 or 8 of cable panel.
BO all sts.

Sleeves
Place held 39 (45, 47, 51, 55, 61, 65, 67, 69) sts of sleeve onto dpns or long circ (if doing magic loop).
Starting at center of underarm sts that were cast on, pick up and knit 4 (4, 4, 4, 5, 5, 5, 5, 6) sts, knit across held sleeve sts, pick up and knit remaining 4 (4, 4, 4, 5, 5, 5, 5, 6) underarm sts—47 (53, 55, 59, 65, 71, 75, 77, 81) sts for sleeve.
Place marker for BOR and knit 15 rnds.
Next rnd *dec rnd*: K1, k2tog, knit to last 3 sts, ssk, k1 (2 sts dec'd).
Continue in St st in the rnd and repeat *dec rnd* every 18th (12th, 18th, 18th, 12th, 18th, 18th, 12th, 12th) rnd 2 (3, 2, 2, 3, 2, 2, 3, 3) times more—41 (45, 49, 53, 57, 65, 69, 69, 73) sts remain.
Continue in St st for another 36 rnds. Sleeve meas approx 13 ¾" [35 cm].
Next rnd *dec rnd*: K1, k2tog, knit to end of rnd (1 st dec'd)—40 (44, 48, 52, 56, 64, 68, 68, 72) sts remain.
Next rnd: *K2, P2; rep from * around.
Repeat the last rnd 27 more times.
BO all sts.

Finishing
Weave in ends and close up any holes at underarms. Soak garment in cool water using a gentle wool wash for 20 minutes. Block garment.

Key

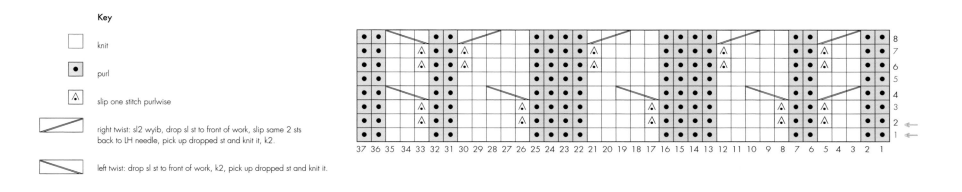

☐   knit

●   purl

⬛   slip one stitch purlwise

◢   right twist: sl2 wyib, drop sl st to front of work, slip same 2 sts back to LH needle, pick up dropped st and knit it, k2.

◢   left twist: drop sl st to front of work, k2, pick up dropped st and knit it.

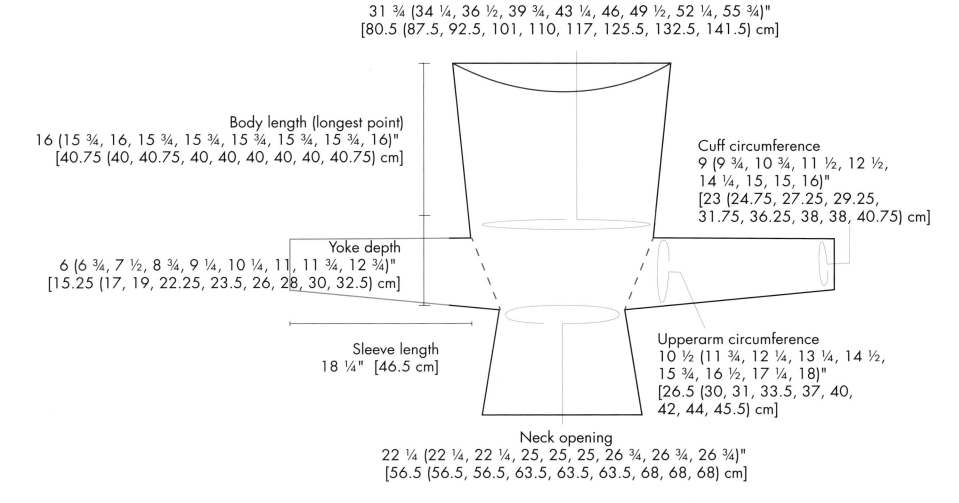

Chest circumference
31 ¾ (34 ¼, 36 ½, 39 ¾, 43 ¼, 46, 49 ½, 52 ¼, 55 ¾)"
[80.5 (87.5, 92.5, 101, 110, 117, 125.5, 132.5, 141.5) cm]

Body length (longest point)
16 (15 ¾, 16, 15 ¾, 15 ¾, 15 ¾, 15 ¾, 15 ¾, 16)"
[40.75 (40, 40.75, 40, 40, 40, 40, 40, 40.75) cm]

Cuff circumference
9 (9 ¾, 10 ¾, 11 ½, 12 ½, 14 ¼, 15, 15, 16)"
[23 (24.75, 27.25, 29.25, 31.75, 36.25, 38, 38, 40.75) cm]

Yoke depth
6 (6 ¾, 7 ½, 8 ¾, 9 ¼, 10 ¼, 11, 11 ¾, 12 ¾)"
[15.25 (17, 19, 22.25, 23.5, 26, 28, 30, 32.5) cm]

Sleeve length
18 ¼" [46.5 cm]

Upperarm circumference
10 ½ (11 ¾, 12 ¼, 13 ¼, 14 ½, 15 ¾, 16 ½, 17 ¼, 18)"
[26.5 (30, 31, 33.5, 37, 40, 42, 44, 45.5) cm]

Neck opening
22 ¼ (22 ¼, 22 ¼, 25, 25, 25, 26 ¾, 26 ¾, 26 ¾)"
[56.5 (56.5, 56.5, 63.5, 63.5, 63.5, 68, 68, 68) cm]

Soay

This cardigan is worked bottom up in one piece, dividing at the armholes to work fronts and back separately. The sleeves are knitted seamlessly by picking up stitches around the armhole and working short rows to shape the cap. The button bands and neck are finished with a clean i-cord bind off.

Finished measurements
29 ½ (31 ½, 33, 35, 36 ¼, 38 ¼, 40 ¼, 42 ¼, 44 ¼, 46 ¼, 48 ¼, 50 ¼)" [75 (80, 84, 89, 92, 97, 102, 107.5, 112.5, 117.5, 122.5, 127.5) cm] bust circumference, closed
Shown in size 29 ½" [75 cm] with ½" negative ease and in size 35" [89 cm] with 1 ½" of negative ease.

Yarn
Chickadee by Quince & Co.
(100% American wool; 181 yd [166 m] / 50 g)
• 4 (5, 5, 5, 5, 6, 6, 7, 7, 7, 8, 8) skeins Pomegranate 112 or Honey 123
  Or 700 (750, 800, 850, 900, 950, 1050, 1100, 1150, 1250, 1300, 1400) yd sport weight yarn.

Needles
• One 16" and 32" circular needle (circ) in size US 5 [3.75 mm]
• One set of double-pointed needles (dpns) in size US 5 [3.75 mm] or one 40" circ if using magic loop to work sleeves
• One 32" circ in size US 4 [3.5 mm]
• One set dpns in size US 4 [3.5 mm]
Or size to obtain gauge

Notions
• Stitch markers (m)
• Tapestry needle
• Waste yarn
• Five ⁵⁄₈" buttons

Gauge
24 sts and 36 rows = 4" [10 cm] in stockinette st with larger needles, after blocking.
26 sts and 36 rows = 4" [10 cm] in rib pattern with larger needles, gently stretched.

Sweater

Begin at hem

Note: Two different cast on methods are used to set up for the ribbing. It is possible to cast on only using the long-tail cast on if you prefer.

Using larger, longer circ, CO 179 (189, 199, 209, 219, 229, 244, 254, 264, 274, 284, 294) sts as follows:

CO 3 sts using a long-tail cast on, CO 3 sts using the German twisted cast on (see techniques), then *CO 2 sts using a long-tail cast on, CO 3 sts using German twisted cast on; repeat from * until 176 (186, 196, 206, 216, 226, 241, 251, 261, 271, 281, 291) sts have been cast on, then CO 3 more sts using a long-tail cast on.

Establish rib pattern

Row 1: (WS) P3, k3, (p2, k3) to last 3 sts, p3.
Row 2: (RS) K3, p3, (k2, p3) to last 3 sts, k3.
Repeat Rows 1–2 seven times more.

Note: The next row sets up markers for the two front lace sections and side seams. The first and last markers separate out the lace sections and the two inside markers delineate the side seams.

Next row *place markers*: (WS) Work Row 1 of rib pattern for 31 sts, pm, work 12 (15, 17, 20, 22, 25, 29, 31, 34, 36, 39, 41) sts, pm, work 93 (97, 103, 107, 113, 117, 124, 130, 134, 140, 144, 150) sts, pm, work 12 (15, 17, 20, 22, 25, 29, 31, 34, 36, 39, 41) sts, pm, work in patt to end.

Note: When working the next row, work decreases in purl bands as p2tog.

Next row *dec row*: (RS) Work in rib pattern as est to first marker, sl m, dec 2 (2, 2, 2, 2, 2, 3, 3, 3, 3, 3, 3) sts as evenly as possible to next marker, sl m, dec 6 (4, 6, 4, 6, 4, 6, 8, 6, 8, 6, 8) sts as evenly as possible across back to next marker, sl m, dec 2 (2, 2, 2, 2, 2, 3, 3, 3, 3, 3, 3) sts as evenly as possible to last marker, sl m, work in rib to end [10 (8, 10, 8, 10, 8, 12, 14, 12, 14, 12, 14) sts dec'd]—41 (44, 46, 49, 51, 54, 57, 59, 62, 64, 67, 69) sts for each front , 87 (93, 97, 103, 107, 113, 118, 122, 128, 132, 138, 142) sts for back,169 (181, 189, 201, 209, 221, 232, 240, 252, 260, 272, 280) total sts.
Next row: (WS) Purl.

Body

Note: Use the lace chart to work the first and last 31 sts of body. All other sts are worked in St st. Once all 48 rows of chart have been worked, then all sts of body are worked in St st.

Beginning with a RS row, work for 6 rows, following the chart for marked out lace portions.

Next row *dec row:* (RS) Continue working first and last 31 sts from lace chart **AND AT THE SAME TIME** dec at side seams by *working to 3 sts before side seam marker, ssk, k1, sl m, k1, k2tog; rep from * for other side seam (4 sts dec'd)—165 (177, 185, 197, 205, 217, 228, 236, 248, 256, 268, 276).
Continue to work from lace chart and repeat *dec row* every 8th (8th, 8th, 8th, 8th, 8th, 6th, 8th, 6th, 8th, 8th, 8th) row 3 (3, 3, 3, 3, 3, 4, 3, 4, 3, 3, 3) times more—153 (165, 173, 185, 193, 205, 212, 224, 232, 244, 256, 264) sts remain.

Work 7 rows as est.

Next row *inc row*: (RS) Knit to 1 st before marker, M1R, k1, sl m, k1, M1L; rep from * once more, knit to end (4 sts inc'd)— 157 (169, 177, 189, 197, 209, 216, 228, 236, 248, 260, 268) sts.
Continue in pattern as est and repeat *inc row* every 6th row 4 (4, 4, 4, 4, 4, 5, 5, 6, 6, 6, 7) times more—173 (185, 193, 205, 213, 225, 236, 248, 260, 272, 284, 296) sts remain.
Work in St st for another 17 (17, 17, 21, 21, 21, 19, 19, 17, 17, 17, 15) rows, ending with a WS row.

Divide for fronts and back

Beginning with a RS row, k38 (41, 42, 45, 46, 49, 51, 53, 55, 57, 59, 61) sts for right front. Place the next 8 (8, 10, 10, 12, 12, 14, 16, 18, 20, 22, 24) sts on a piece of waste yarn for underarm (leaving marker in place) and either leave the remaining sts on the longer circular or place them onto a separate piece of waste yarn to be worked later.

Right front

Turn work and purl one WS row.

Shape armhole and neck

Dec 1 st for armhole shaping at the end of each RS row 4 (4, 5, 5, 6, 6, 7, 7, 8, 8, 9, 9) times as follows: Work to last 3 sts, k2tog, k1, **AND AT THE SAME TIME,** shape front neck as follows:
Dec 1 st at neck edge EVERY row (by working k1, ssk over the first 3 sts on RS rows and ssp, p1 over the last 3 sts on WS rows) for a total of 20 (20, 20, 22, 22, 24, 24, 26, 26, 28, 28, 28) rows—14 (17, 17, 18, 18, 19, 20, 20, 21, 21, 22, 24) sts remain for shoulder.

Once armhole and neck shaping are finished, work even in St st for another 34 (36, 40, 38, 42, 40, 42, 40, 44, 44, 46, 50) rows, ending with a WS row.

Begin shoulder shaping
Note: See abbreviations for how to work w&t.
Short Row 1: Knit to last 4 (4, 6, 6, 6, 6, 7, 7, 7, 7, 7, 8) sts, w&t, purl to end.
Short Row 2: Knit to 4 (4, 6, 6, 6, 6, 7, 7, 7, 7, 7, 8) sts before previous wrap, w&t, purl to end.
Knit 1 row and pick up wraps.
Cut yarn and place sts on waste yarn.

Left front
Beginning at the center front edge of left front, slip 38 (41, 42, 45, 46, 49, 51, 53, 55, 57, 59, 61) sts onto the larger, longer circ. Place the next 8 (8, 10,10, 12, 12, 14, 16, 18, 20, 22, 24) sts on a piece of waste yarn for underarm (leaving marker in place) and either leave the remaining sts on the longer circular or place them onto a separate piece of waste yarn to be worked later.
Re-join yarn at the underarm edge with RS facing.
Knit 1 row.
Purl 1 row.

Begin armhole and neck shaping
Beginning on next row, dec 1 st at the beginning of each RS row 4 (4, 5, 5, 6, 6, 7, 7, 8, 8, 9, 9) times as follows: k1, ssk, knit to end of row **AND AT THE SAME TIME**, shape front neck as follows:
Dec 1 st at neck edge EVERY row (by working k2tog, k1 over last 3 sts on RS rows and p1, p2tog on first 3 sts on WS rows) for a total of 20 (20, 20, 22, 22, 24, 24, 26, 26, 28, 28, 28) rows—14 (17, 17, 18, 18, 19, 20, 20, 21, 21, 22, 24) sts remain for shoulder.

Continue in St st for another 33 (35, 39, 37, 41, 39, 41, 39, 43, 43, 45, 49) rows, ending with a RS row.

Begin shoulder shaping
Short Row 1: Purl to last 4 (4, 6, 6, 6, 6, 7, 7, 7, 7, 7, 8) sts, w&t, knit to end.
Short Row 2: Purl to 4 (4, 6, 6, 6, 6, 7, 7, 7, 7, 7, 8) sts before previous wrap, w&t, knit to end.
Purl 1 row and pick up wraps.
Knit 1 row.
Cut yarn and place sts on waste yarn.

Back
Re-join yarn to 81 (87, 89, 95, 97, 103, 106, 110, 114, 118, 123, 126) sts of back with RS facing.
Knit 1 row.
Purl 1 row.

Shape armholes
Next row *dec row*: (RS) K1, ssk, knit to last 3 sts, k2tog, k1 (2 sts dec'd).
Continue in St st and repeat *dec row* every RS row 3 (3, 4, 4, 5, 5, 6, 6, 7, 7, 8, 8) times more—73 (79, 79, 85, 85, 91, 92, 96, 98, 102, 104, 108) sts remain.
Continue in St st for another 41 (43, 45, 45, 47, 47, 47, 47, 49, 51, 51, 55) rows, ending with a WS row.

Shape back neck
Row 1: (RS) Knit 16 (19, 19, 20, 20, 21, 22, 22, 23, 23, 24, 26) sts, join new yarn and bind off 41 (41, 41, 45, 45, 49, 48, 52, 52, 56, 56, 56) sts at center back, knit to end.
Row 2: Working each side separately, purl 1 WS row across each shoulder.
Continue in St st and dec 1 st at each neck edge on the next 2 RS rows as follows: knit to 3 sts before neck edge, k2tog, k1; on other side, k1, ssk, knit to end—14 (17, 17, 18, 18, 19, 20, 20, 21, 21, 22, 24) sts remain for each shoulder.

Now working each shoulder separately:
Back left shoulder
Purl 1 row.
Short Row 1: Knit to last 4 (4, 6, 6, 6, 6, 7, 7, 7, 7, 7, 8) sts, w&t, purl to end.
Short Row 2: Knit to 4 (4, 6, 6, 6, 6, 7, 7, 7, 7, 7, 8) sts before previous wrap, w&t, purl to end.
Knit 1 row and pick up wraps.
Cut yarn and place sts on waste yarn.

Back right shoulder
Short Row 1: Purl to last 4 (4, 6, 6, 6, 6, 7, 7, 7, 7, 7, 8) sts, w&t, knit to end.
Short Row 2: Purl to 4 (4, 6, 6, 6, 6, 7, 7, 7, 7, 7, 8) sts before previous wrap, w&t, knit to end.
Purl 1 row and pick up wraps.
Knit 1 row.
Cut yarn and leave sts on needle.

Join shoulders

Place sts of right front shoulder onto larger, shorter circ. Holding the right back shoulder sts and right front shoulder sts with right sides facing and using tail of yarn already in place, join sts of right front shoulder with right back shoulder using the three needle bind off.

Repeat the shoulder join with the left front shoulder and left back shoulder sts.

Sleeves

Note: Sleeves are worked by picking up sts from the armhole and working short rows to shape the sleeve cap. The ratio for picking up sts around the armhole is about 1 out of every 2 rows.

Using the larger, shorter circ or dpns, place the 4 (4, 5, 5, 6, 6, 7, 8, 9, 10, 11, 12) underarm sts to the left of the marker on the needle, re-join yarn and knit across these, then pick up 28 (29, 31, 31, 33, 33, 34, 34, 36, 37, 38, 40) sts to shoulder join, pm, then pick up and knit 28 (29, 31, 31, 33, 33, 34, 34, 36, 37, 38, 40) sts back down the other side to underarm sts, place next 4 (4, 5, 5, 6, 6, 7, 8, 9, 10, 11, 12) underarm sts to the right of the marker on the left hand needle and knit across these. Marker delineates beginning of rnd—64 (66, 72, 72, 78, 78, 82, 84, 90, 94, 98, 104) sts for sleeve.

Shape sleeve cap

Note: See abbreviations for how to work w&t.

Short Row 1: (RS) Knit to 5 sts past shoulder seam marker, w&t.
Short Row 2: (WS) Purl to 5 sts past shoulder seam marker, w&t.
Short Row 3: Knit to wrapped st, work wrap with the st it wraps, w&t.
Short Row 4: Purl to wrapped st, work wrap with the st it wraps, w&t.
Repeat Short Rows 3–4 until all sts except the underarm sts have been worked.
After last w&t on a WS row, knit to end of rnd, picking up the wrapped st as you come to it.
Knit 1 rnd and pick up the final wrapped stitch (as for a RS row).

Note: If you feel the picked up sts around the armhole look too loose then try the following method for tightening them up: Pull firmly on the tail of the pick up yarn (which will be hanging from the center of the underarm), being very careful not to pull too aggressively, or the armscythe will become too tight. Instead pull a bit at a time and then carefully even out the cinched up stitches.

Next rnd *dec rnd*: K1, k2tog, knit to last 3 sts, ssk, k1 (2 sts dec'd).
Continue knitting every rnd and repeat *dec rnd* every 10th (8th, 6th, 6th, 6th, 6th, 6th, 6th, 6th, 6th, 6th, 6th) rnd 3 (4, 5, 5, 5, 5, 5, 6, 6, 6, 6, 6) times more, changing to larger dpns as necessary—56 (56, 60, 60, 66, 66, 70, 70, 76, 80, 86, 90) sts remain.

Knit 8 (6, 8, 8, 8, 8, 8, 2, 2, 2, 2, 2) rnds more **AND AT THE SAME TIME** on the last rnd dec 1 (1, 0, 0, 1, 1, 0, 0, 1, 0, 1, 0) st more by working a k2tog at the beginning of the rnd—55 (55, 60, 60, 65, 65, 70, 70, 75, 80, 85, 90) sts remain.

Change to smaller dpns.
Work in k2, p3 rib for 4 rnds.
Bind off all sts in rib.

Button band

Note: Specific numbers have been given for number of sts to pick up for buttonbands, however it does not matter if you end up with a slightly different amount. Ratio for picking up sts is approx 3 out of every 4 rows.

Using smaller circ, and beginning at neck edge of left front (where neck shaping begins) with RS facing, pick up and knit 74 (74, 74, 77, 77, 77, 80, 80, 83, 83, 83, 86) sts down left front.
Work in St st for 5 rows, ending with a WS row.
Cut yarn and place sts on waste yarn.

Buttonhole band

Using smaller circ, and beginning at hem edge of right front with RS facing, pick up and knit 74 (74, 74, 77, 77, 77, 80, 80, 83, 83, 83, 86) sts up right front to beg of neck shaping.
Row 1: (WS) Purl.
Row 2: Knit.
Row 3 *buttonhole row*: P3 (3, 3, 4, 4, 4, 4, 4, 3, 3, 3, 3), yo, p2tog, *p14 (14, 14, 14, 14, 14, 15, 15, 16, 16, 16, 17), yo, p2tog; rep from * four times more, knit to end.
Row 4: Knit.
Row 5: Purl.
Leave sts on needle.

I-cord bind off

Note: An i-cord bind off is worked up the right front, around neck and down the left front. For the neck band section you will be picking up sts and working an i-cord bind off simultaneously.

Soay lace chart

left front   right front

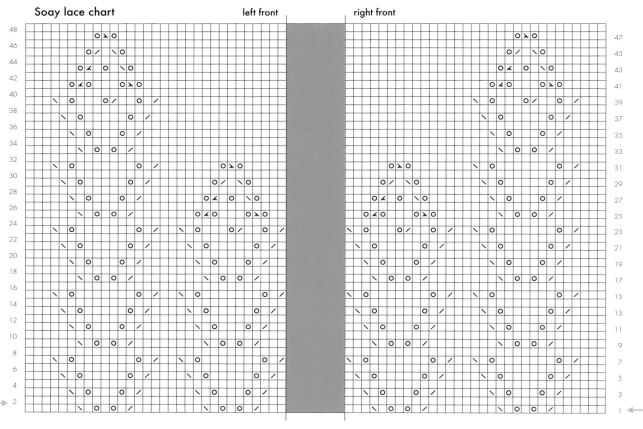

Key

- ☐ knit on RS, purl on WS
- ╱ k2tog
- ╲ ssk
- ⊙ yo
- ⊼ k3tog
- ⋏ sk2p
- ▨ sts between markers of right front and left front lace; work in St st
- │ marker position

I-cord for buttonhole band

Begin by casting on 2 sts.
With RS of work facing, work the i-cord bind off as follows: *k2, ssk, slip 3 sts on RH needle back to LH needle; repeat from * until all sts from right front button band have been worked, leaving 3 sts on RH needle.

I-cord for neck

Note: The ratio for picking up sts around the neck band section is as follows—
1:1 across top of buttonhole band, 1:1 across shaped portion of right front neck, 3:4 up right front neck and down back neck, 1:1 across bound off sts of back neck, 3:4 up left back neck and down left front neck, 1:1 across shaped portion of left front neck, 1:1 across button band.
*Using the RH needle, pick up and knit 1 st from top edge of buttonhole band, slip 4 sts on RH needle to LH needle, k2, ssk; repeat from *, picking up sts using the ratios given until you reach the held sts of left button band.

I-cord for button band

Place sts of left button band back on needle and work i-cord bind off as for buttonhole band until all sts from left front have been used; there should be 3 sts left on RH needle.
Slip last 3 sts back to LH needle and work sk2p.
Cut yarn and draw through remaining loop.

Finishing

Weave in ends and sew up any holes that may be noticeable at the underarms.
Block garment.
Attach buttons opposite buttonholes.

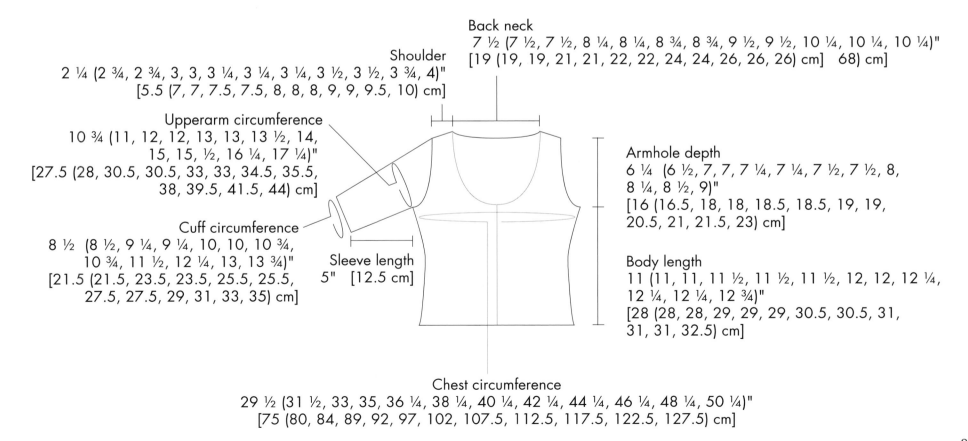

Back neck
7 ½ (7 ½, 7 ½, 8 ¼, 8 ¼, 8 ¾, 8 ¾, 9 ½, 9 ½, 10 ¼, 10 ¼, 10 ¼)"
[19 (19, 19, 21, 21, 22, 22, 24, 24, 26, 26, 26) cm]   68) cm]

Shoulder
2 ¼ (2 ¾, 2 ¾, 3, 3, 3 ¼, 3 ¼, 3 ¼, 3 ½, 3 ½, 3 ¾, 4)"
[5.5 (7, 7, 7.5, 7.5, 8, 8, 8, 9, 9, 9.5, 10) cm]

Upperarm circumference
10 ¾ (11, 12, 12, 13, 13, 13 ½, 14, 15, 15, ½, 16 ¼, 17 ¼)"
[27.5 (28, 30.5, 30.5, 33, 33, 34.5, 35.5, 38, 39.5, 41.5, 44) cm]

Cuff circumference
8 ½ (8 ½, 9 ¼, 9 ¼, 10, 10, 10 ¾, 10 ¾, 11 ½, 12 ¼, 13, 13 ¾)"
[21.5 (21.5, 23.5, 23.5, 25.5, 25.5, 27.5, 27.5, 29, 31, 33, 35) cm]

Sleeve length
5"   [12.5 cm]

Armhole depth
6 ¼ (6 ½, 7, 7, 7 ¼, 7 ¼, 7 ½, 7 ½, 8, 8 ¼, 8 ½, 9)"
[16 (16.5, 18, 18, 18.5, 18.5, 19, 19, 20.5, 21, 21.5, 23) cm]

Body length
11 (11, 11, 11 ½, 11 ½, 11 ½, 12, 12, 12 ¼, 12 ¼, 12 ¼, 12 ¾)"
[28 (28, 28, 29, 29, 29, 30.5, 30.5, 31, 31, 31, 32.5) cm]

Chest circumference
29 ½ (31 ½, 33, 35, 36 ¼, 38 ¼, 40 ¼, 42 ¼, 44 ¼, 46 ¼, 48 ¼, 50 ¼)"
[75 (80, 84, 89, 92, 97, 102, 107.5, 112.5, 117.5, 122.5, 127.5) cm]

McIntosh

This simple, open-front cardigan is worked as a top-down raglan. The fronts at the bottom edge are shaped using short rows and finished with an i-cord bind off. The ribbing is worked by picking up stitches around the fronts and back neck.

Finished measurements
30 ½ (33 ¼, 36, 39 ¼, 42, 44 ½, 47 ¼, 50, 53 ¼, 56)" [77.5 (84.5, 91.5, 99.5, 106.5, 113, 120, 127, 135, 142) cm] bust circumference
Shown in 36" [91.5 cm] and 39 ¼" [99.5 cm] with 2 ¾" positive ease.

Yarn
Chickadee by Quince & Co.
 (100% American wool; 181 yd [166 m] / 50 g)
- 4 (4, 5, 5, 5, 6, 6, 6, 7, 7) skeins in Kittywake 151 or Frost 103 (MC)
- 2 (2, 2, 3, 3, 3, 3, 3, 4, 4) skeins in Kumlien's Gull 152 or Bird's Egg 106 (CC)
  Or 667 (704, 765, 816, 882, 930, 1000, 1042, 1121, 1164) yd in MC and 290 (328, 350, 395, 419, 467, 490, 540, 567, 618) yd in CC in sport weight yarn.
  Samples shown in Kittywake/Kumlien's Gull (36") and Frost/Bird's Egg (39 ¼")

Needles
- One 32" or 40" circular needle (circ) in size US 5 [3.75mm]
- One 32" or 40" circ US 4 [3.5mm]
- One set of double-pointed needles (dpns) in size US 5 [3.75mm] or use longest circ to work magic loop for sleeves

Or size to obtain gauge

Notions
- Stitch markers (m)
- Stitch holders or waste yarn
- Tapestry needle for weaving in ends
- Twelve 4" strips of CC yarn in a similar weight to working yarn

Gauge
24 sts and 36 rows = 4" [10 cm] in stockinette st on larger needles, after blocking.

Cardigan
Shape yoke

Using larger, longer circ and CC, CO 68 (72, 74, 78, 80, 88, 90, 94, 98, 102) sts.

Set up row *place markers*: (WS) P3 for left front, pm, p10 (10, 10, 10, 10, 12, 12, 12, 12, 12) for sleeve, pm, p42 (46, 48, 52, 54, 58, 60, 64, 68, 72) for back, pm, p10 (10, 10, 10, 10, 12, 12, 12, 12, 12) for sleeve, pm, p3 for right front (4 raglan markers placed).

Next row *inc row*: (RS) Knit to 2 sts before m, k1-r/b, k1, sl m, k1, k1-r/b; repeat from * three times more (8 sts inc'd)—76 (80, 82, 86, 88, 96, 98, 102, 106, 110) sts.

Next row: Purl.

Change to MC and rep last two rows 22 (24, 26, 28, 30, 32, 34, 36, 38, 40) times more, changing colors every 4 rows (Note: When changing colors, do not cut yarn each time. Instead, carry color not being used up side of work by twisting it around other color at the beginning of RS rows)—252 (272, 290, 310, 328, 352, 370, 390, 410, 430) sts total: 88 (96, 102, 110, 116, 124, 130, 138, 146, 154) sts for back, 56 (60, 64, 68, 72, 78, 82, 86, 90, 94) sts for sleeves, 26 (28, 30, 32, 34, 36, 38, 40, 42, 44) sts for each front.

Divide body and sleeves

Knit to first m, remove m, place next 56 (60, 64, 68, 72, 78, 82, 86, 90, 94) sts of sleeve on waste yarn, and using the backward loop cast on, CO 4 (4, 6, 8, 10, 10, 12, 12, 14, 14) sts, knit across sts of back to next m, remove m, place next 56 (60, 64, 68, 72, 78, 82, 86, 90, 94) sts of 2nd sleeve on waste yarn, and using the backward loop cast on, CO 4 (4, 6, 8, 10, 10, 12, 12, 14, 14) sts, knit to end—148 (160, 174, 190, 204, 216, 230, 242, 258, 270) sts for body.

Continue in St st, keeping the same stripe sequence for another 107 (111, 107, 111, 107, 111, 107, 111, 107, 111) rows. End with a WS row and a CC stripe.

Work 18 (14, 18, 14, 18, 14, 18, 14, 18, 14) rows in MC.

Short rows to shape fronts

Before beginning short row section, cut twelve 4" strips of CC yarn.

Left front

Short Row 1: K25, turn work, place one strip of contrast yarn across working yarn as for a Sunday Short Row (see techniques), purl to end.

Short Row 2: Knit to 2 sts before previous turning point, turn work, place one strip of contrast yarn across working yarn, purl to end.

Repeat Short Row 2 ten times more.

12 strips of contrast yarn will have been placed at the turning points.

Knit across entire row, working the turning points as described for Sunday Short Rows (see techniques).

Right front

Short Row 1: P25, turn work, place one strip of contrast yarn across working yarn as for a Sunday Short Row (see techniques), knit to end.

Short Row 2: Purl to 2 sts before previous turning point, turn work, place one strip of contrast yarn across working yarn, knit to end.

Repeat Short Row 2 ten times more.

12 strips of contrast yarn will have been placed at the turning points.

Purl across entire row, working the turning points as described for Sunday Short Rows (see techniques).

Place body sts on waste yarn to be worked later.

Sleeves

Using dpns or larger, longer circ (if working magic loop) and beginning with the next color in the stripe sequence for sleeves, start at the center of the cast on underarm sts and pick up and knit 2 (2, 3, 4, 5, 5, 6, 6, 7, 7) underarm sts, knit across 56 (60, 64, 68, 72, 78, 82, 86, 90, 94) held sts of sleeve, then pick up and knit remaining 2 (2, 3, 4, 5, 5, 6, 6, 7, 7) underarm sts. Pm for BOR and join to work in the rnd—60 (64, 70, 76, 82, 88, 94, 98, 104, 108) sts total.

Work even in St st, keeping in stripe sequence as est, for 7 rnds.

Next rnd *dec rnd*: K1, k2tog, knit to 3 sts before end of rnd, ssk, k1 (2 sts decreased).

Continue in St st in the rnd, keeping in stripe sequence as est, and repeat *dec rnd* every 8th rnd 0 (0, 2, 4, 8, 9, 9, 9, 10, 10) times, then every 12th rnd 3 (3, 3, 3, 0, 0, 0, 0, 0, 0) times—52 (56, 58, 60, 64, 68, 74, 78, 82, 86) sts remain.

Work even for 48 (52, 32, 20, 20, 16, 12, 16, 4, 8) rnds, ending with a CC stripe.

Work even for 18 (14, 18, 14, 18, 14, 18, 14, 18, 14) rnds in MC.

Next rnd: *K1, p1; rep from * to end of rnd.

Repeat last rnd 3 more times.

BO all sts in pattern.

Front bands

Note: When picking up sts for the front band, make sure to pick up a full stitch in from the edge for the best join. Exact numbers of sts to pick up are not given but the ratios for each section are described, however an odd number of sts are required to work the front bands.

Using smaller, longer circ and starting at bottom edge of right front, pick up and knit at a ratio of 3:4 rows up to back neck sts, pick up and knit at a ratio of 1:1 on neck sts, then 3:4 down left front.
Make sure you have an odd number of sts.

Next row: (WS) *P1, k1; rep from * to last st, p1.
Next row: (RS) *K1, p1; rep from * to last st, k1.
Rep last two rows 9 times more, then work one more WS row in pattern.
21 rows worked total.
BO all sts in pattern.

Hem

Using larger circ and MC, start at bottom left corner and pick up and knit 16 sts across bottom edge of left front band (picking up at a ratio of 3:4 rows), place held sts of body onto needle and knit across these, then pick up and knit 16 sts from bottom edge of right front band.
Next row: (WS) Knit.

Work i-cord bind off across all sts as follows:
Begin by casting on 2 sts using the backward loop cast on.
With RS of work facing, *k2, ssk, slip 3 sts from RH needle back to LH needle; rep from * until you have 3 sts remaining on the LH needle, sk2p, cut yarn leaving tail and draw through remaining st.

Finishing
Weave in ends.
Soak garment in cool water using a gentle wool wash for 20 minutes.
Block garment.

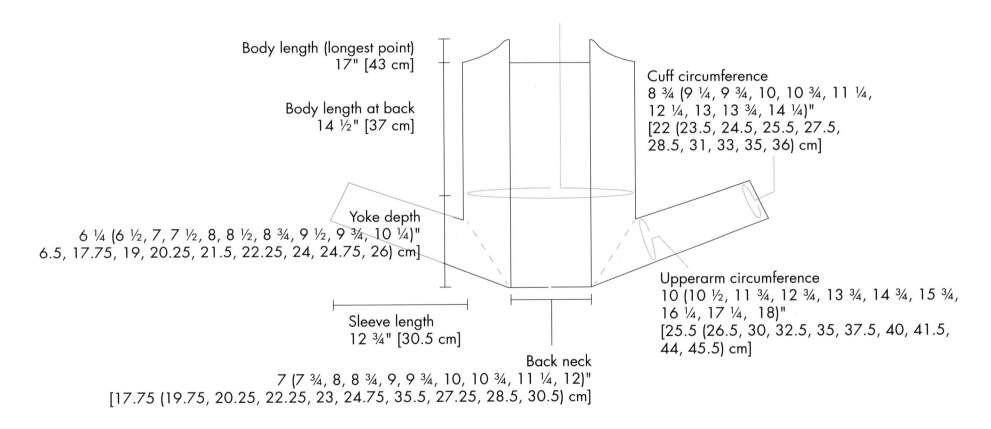

Chest circumference
30 ½ (33 ¼, 36, 39 ¼, 42, 44 ½, 47 ¼, 50, 53 ¼, 56)"
[77.5 (84.5, 91.5, 99.5, 106.5, 113, 120, 127, 135, 142) cm]

Body length (longest point)
17" [43 cm]

Body length at back
14 ½" [37 cm]

Cuff circumference
8 ¾ (9 ¼, 9 ¾, 10, 10 ¾, 11 ¼,
12 ¼, 13, 13 ¾, 14 ¼)"
[22 (23.5, 24.5, 25.5, 27.5,
28.5, 31, 33, 35, 36) cm]

Yoke depth

6 ¼ (6 ½, 7, 7 ½, 8, 8 ½, 8 ¾, 9 ½, 9 ¾, 10 ¼)"
6.5, 17.75, 19, 20.25, 21.5, 22.25, 24, 24.75, 26) cm]

Upperarm circumference
10 (10 ½, 11 ¾, 12 ¾, 13 ¾, 14 ¾, 15 ¾,
16 ¼, 17 ¼, 18)"
[25.5 (26.5, 30, 32.5, 35, 37.5, 40, 41.5,
44, 45.5) cm]

Sleeve length
12 ¾" [30.5 cm]

Back neck
7 (7 ¾, 8, 8 ¾, 9, 9 ¾, 10, 10 ¾, 11 ¼, 12)"
[17.75 (19.75, 20.25, 22.25, 23, 24.75, 35.5, 27.25, 28.5, 30.5) cm]

Brock

This cardigan is worked top down and features a pretty seed stitch chevron pattern at the yoke. The lower body is shaped using short rows creating a delicate curve at the hem. The ¾ length sleeves gently bell out and are then brought back in with decreases at the cuff.

Finished measurements
31 (33 ½, 36 ¼, 38 ¼, 40 ¼, 42 ¼, 45, 47, 49, 52 ¼)" [78.5 (85, 92, 97, 102, 107.5, 114, 119.5, 124.5, 132.5) cm] bust circumference, closed
Shown in 33 ½" [85 cm] and 38 ¼" [97 cm] with 2 ¼" positive ease.

Yarn
Tern by Quince & Co.
(75% American wool/25% silk; 221 yd [202 m] / 50 g)
• 4 (5, 5, 5, 6, 6, 6, 7, 7, 7) skeins, shown in Oyster 142 and Boothbay Blue 145
Or 880 (960, 1040, 1100, 1160, 1210, 1290, 1350, 1400, 1500) yd fingering weight yarn.

Needles
• One 24", 32", and 40" circular needle (circ) in size US 5 [3.75 mm]
• One set double-pointed needles (dpns) in size US 5 [3.75 mm] or use longest circ to work magic loop for sleeves
• One crochet hook in size US D-3 [3.25 mm]
Or size to obtain gauge

Notions
• Stitch markers (m)
• Stitch holders or waste yarn
• Three ½" buttons
• Tapestry needle
• Twenty 4" strips of a CC yarn in a similar weight to working yarn

Gauge
24 sts and 35 rows =4" [10 cm] in stockinette st, after blocking.

Cardigan
Begin at yoke
Using shortest circ and the long-tail cast on, CO 147 (147, 147, 165, 165, 165, 183, 183, 183, 201) sts.

Set up row: (WS) Purl.

Work Rows 1–42 of charts.

Note: The repeated section of the charts is worked 8 (8, 8, 9, 9, 9, 10, 10, 10, 11) times per row.

16 (16, 16, 18, 18, 18, 20, 20, 20, 22) sts will be increased on rows 9, 25 and 33:

163 (163, 163, 183, 183, 183, 203, 203, 223) sts after row 9.

179 (179, 179, 201, 201, 201, 223, 223, 223, 245) sts after row 25.

195 (195, 195, 219, 219, 219, 243, 243, 243, 267) sts after row 33.

Next row *inc row*: (RS) K13, M1R, k1, M1L, [k23, M1R, k1, M1L] 7 (7, 7, 8, 8, 8, 9, 9, 9, 10) times, knit to end [16 (16, 16, 18, 18, 18, 20, 20, 20, 22) sts inc'd]—211 (211, 211, 237, 237, 237, 263, 263, 263, 289) sts.

Begin raglan shaping
Setup row *place markers*: (WS) P34 (34, 34, 37, 37, 37, 40, 40, 40, 43), pm, p36 (36, 36, 43, 43, 43, 50, 50, 50, 57), pm, p71 (71, 71, 77, 77, 77, 83, 83, 83, 89), pm, p36 (36, 36, 43, 43, 43, 50, 50, 50, 57), pm, P34 (34, 34, 37, 37, 37, 40, 40, 40, 43).

Row 1 *inc row*: (RS) *Knit to 2 sts before marker, k1-r/b, k1, sl m, k1, k1-r/b; rep from * 3 more times, knit to end (8 sts inc'd).

Row 2: Purl.

Rep last two rows 5 (7, 9, 11, 13, 15, 17, 19, 21, 23) times more—259 (275, 291, 333, 349, 365, 407, 423, 439, 481) sts.

Divide for body and sleeves
Next row: (RS) K40 (42, 44, 49, 51, 53, 58, 60, 62, 67) sts of left front, remove m, place next 48 (52, 56, 67, 71, 75, 86, 90, 94, 105) sts on holder or waste yarn for sleeve, and using the backward loop cast on CO 5 (7, 9, 7, 8, 9, 8, 9, 10, 10) sts, pm, CO 5 (7, 9, 7, 8, 9, 8, 9, 10, 10) more sts, then knit across 83 (87, 91, 101, 105, 109, 119, 123, 127, 137) sts of back, remove m, place next 48 (52, 56, 67, 71, 75, 86, 90, 94, 105) sts on holder or waste yarn for sleeve, and using the backward loop cast on CO 5 (7, 9, 7, 8, 9, 8, 9, 10, 10) sts, pm, CO 5 (7, 9, 7, 8, 9, 8, 9, 10, 10) more sts, k40 (42, 44, 49, 51, 53, 58, 60, 62, 67) sts of right front—183 (199, 215, 227, 239, 251, 267, 279, 291, 311) sts for body (2 side markers placed).

Continue in St st for 11 (11, 11, 13, 13, 13, 15, 15, 15, 15) more rows, ending on a WS row.

Begin side shaping
Next row *inc row*: (RS) *Knit to 2 sts before marker, k1-r/b, k1, sl m, k1, k1-r/b; rep from * once more knit to end (4 sts inc'd).

Continue in St st and repeat *inc row* every 10th row once more, then every 14th row twice more—199 (215, 231, 243, 255, 267, 283, 295, 307, 327) sts.

Work 5 (5, 5, 7, 7, 7, 9, 9, 9, 9) rows in St st, ending with a WS row.

Begin front shaping short rows
Short Row 1: (RS) Knit to 4 (4, 4, 4, 4, 4, 5, 5, 5, 5) sts before end of row, turn work, place one strip of CC yarn across working yarn as for a Sunday Short Row (see techniques).

Short Row 2: Purl to 4 (4, 4, 4, 4, 4, 5, 5, 5, 5) sts before end of row, turn work, place one strip of CC yarn across working yarn as for a Sunday Short Row.

Short Row 3: Knit to 4 (4, 4, 4, 4, 4, 5, 5, 5, 5) sts before previous turning point, turn work, place one strip of CC yarn across working yarn.

Short Row 4: Purl to 4 (4, 4, 4, 4, 4, 5, 5, 5, 5) sts before previous turning point, turn work, place one strip of CC yarn across working yarn.

Repeat Short Rows 3–4 eight times more.

After final turning point, knit to end of row and resolve short rows as for a RS row (see techniques).

Purl 1 row and resolve short rows as for a WS row (see techniques).

Next row: (RS) (K1, p1) to last st, k1.

Next row: (WS) (P1, k1) to last st, p1.

Repeat these 2 rows once more.

BO all sts.

Sleeves
Place held sleeve sts onto longest circ (if using magic loop method to work sleeves) or dpns, and starting at center of underarm sts pick up and knit 5 (7, 9, 7, 8, 9, 8, 9, 10, 10) sts, then knit across 48 (52, 56, 67, 71, 75, 86, 90, 94, 105) held sleeve sts, then pick up and knit 5 (7, 9, 7, 8, 9, 8, 9, 10, 10) sts from underarm—58 (66, 74, 81, 87, 93, 102, 108, 114, 125) sts for sleeve.

Place marker for beginning of rnd.

Work in St st in the rnd for 28 rnds; sleeve meas 3 ¼" [8.25 cm].

Next rnd *inc rnd*: K1, k1-r/b, knit to last 2 sts, k1-r/b, k1 (2 sts inc'd).

Continue in St st and repeat *inc rnd* every 8th rnd once, then every 12th rnd three times—68 (76, 84, 91, 97, 103, 112, 118, 124, 135) sts.

Work even in St st for 11 more rnds.

Follow directions for your size, then proceed to All sizes resume.

Size 31"
Next rnd: K2tog, k2 *k2tog, k1; rep from * to last 4 sts, k2tog, k2 (22 sts dec'd)—46 sts remain.

Sizes 33 ½" and 38 ¼"
Next rnd: *K2tog, k1, k2tog; rep from * around to last st, k1 [30 (36) sts dec'd]—46 (55) sts remain.

Size 36 ¼"
Next rnd: K2, *k2tog, k1; rep from * to last 2 sts, k2 (32 sts dec'd)—52 sts remain.

Sizes 40 ¼" and 45"
Next rnd: K1, *k2tog, k1, k2tog; rep from * around to last st, k1 [38 (44) sts dec'd]—59 (68) sts remain.

Sizes 42 ¼" and 47"
Next rnd: K2, *k2tog, k1, k2tog; rep from * around to last st, k1 [40 (46) sts dec'd]—63 (72) sts remain.

Size 49"
Next rnd: K2, *k2tog, k1, k2tog; rep from * around to last 2 sts, k2 (48 sts dec'd)—76 sts remain.

Size 52 ¼"
Next rnd: *K2tog, k1, k2tog; rep from * around (54 sts dec'd)—81 sts remain.

All sizes resume:
Turn work (now working back and forth and not in the rnd), purl 1 row, and at end of row CO 2 sts using the backward loop cast on.
Work I-cord bind off as follows: With RS of work facing, *k2, ssk, slip 3 sts from RH needle back to LH needle; rep from * until you have 3 sts remaining on the LH needle, sk2p, cut yarn leaving tail and draw through remaining st.

Front button bands and neck edging
Using waste yarn in a contrast color, mark out placement for three button loops on right front beginning with one at the top. Place the other two approx 1 ½" [3.75 cm] apart.

Starting at bottom corner of right front and using longest circ, pick up and knit 3 out of 4 rows up right front (the exact number is not important), then pick up each of the CO sts of neck, then pick up 3 out of 4 rows down left front.
Purl 1 WS row, and at end of row CO 2 sts using the backward loop cast on.

Note: The next row will create the i-cord bind off around the fronts and neck. The i-cord is worked a little differently for the top part of the right front and for the neck sts. Make sure to read the whole of the following paragraph carefully before beginning.

Turn work to RS and work i-cord bind off (as for sleeve cuffs) up sts of right front to first button loop marker. Slip 3 sts back as normal (after an ssk) then k1, slip this st just worked onto the crochet hook and chain 8 sts (see techniques) making the first st tight, then slip the st on the crochet hook back to the RH needle, k1, ssk and continue with i-cord bind off normally until next loop marker. Work the next two button loops same as the first. When working the i-cord bind off on the neck sts, work every 12th (12th, 12th, 8th, 8th, 8th, 6th, 6th, 6th, 6th) ssk as an sssk (to tighten up neck a little), then once you reach left front work i-cord bind off as normal to end until you have 3 sts remaining on the LH needle, sk2p, cut yarn leaving tail and draw through remaining st.

Finishing
Weave in ends, join i-cord bind off at cuffs, close any holes at underarms.
Soak garment in cool water using a gentle wool wash for 20 minutes.
Block garment. Sew buttons opposite button loops.

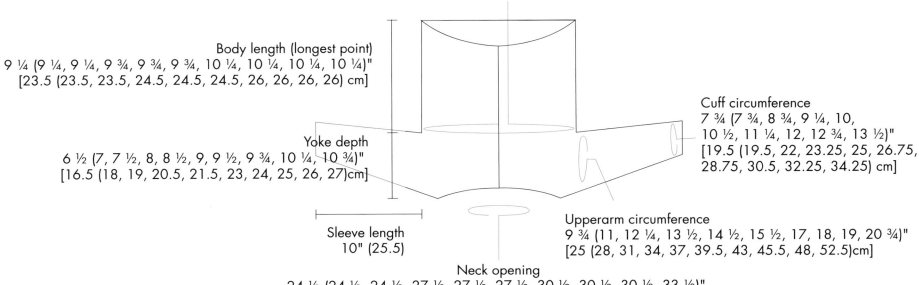

Chest circumference
31 (33 ½, 36 ¼, 38 ¼, 40 ¼, 42 ¼, 45, 47, 49, 52 ¼)"
[78.5 (85, 92, 97, 102, 107.5, 114, 119.5, 124.5, 132.5) cm]

Body length (longest point)
9 ¼ (9 ¼, 9 ¼, 9 ¾, 9 ¾, 9 ¾, 10 ¼, 10 ¼, 10 ¼, 10 ¼)"
[23.5 (23.5, 23.5, 24.5, 24.5, 24.5, 26, 26, 26, 26) cm]

Cuff circumference
7 ¾ (7 ¾, 8 ¾, 9 ¼, 10,
10 ½, 11 ¼, 12, 12 ¾, 13 ½)"
[19.5 (19.5, 22, 23.25, 25, 26.75,
28.75, 30.5, 32.25, 34.25) cm]

Yoke depth
6 ½ (7, 7 ½, 8, 8 ½, 9, 9 ½, 9 ¾, 10 ¼, 10 ¾)"
[16.5 (18, 19, 20.5, 21.5, 23, 24, 25, 26, 27)cm]

Sleeve length
10" (25.5)

Upperarm circumference
9 ¾ (11, 12 ¼, 13 ½, 14 ½, 15 ½, 17, 18, 19, 20 ¾)"
[25 (28, 31, 34, 37, 39.5, 43, 45.5, 48, 52.5)cm]

Neck opening
24 ½ (24 ½, 24 ½, 27 ½, 27 ½, 27 ½, 30 ½, 30 ½, 30 ½, 33 ½)"
[62.25 (62.25, 62.25, 70, 70, 70, 77.5, 77.5, 77.5, 85) cm]

Brock chart: Rows 1-8

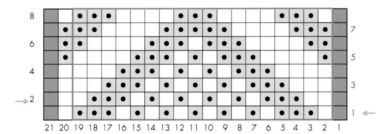

Brock chart: Rows 25-32

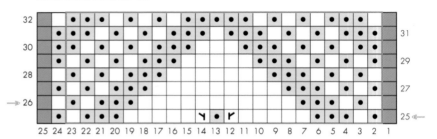

Brock chart: Rows 9-24

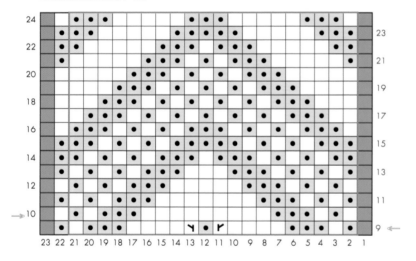

Brock chart: Rows 33-42

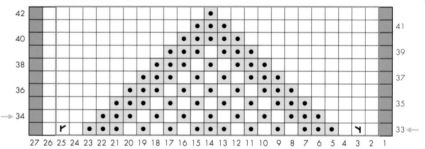

Key

●	purl on RS, knit on WS
↰	M1L
↱	M1R
□	pattern repeat
▨	edge stitch

Empire

This cardigan is worked bottom up in one piece dividing at the armholes to work fronts and back separately. The sleeves are then formed by picking up sts around the armhole and working short rows to shape the caps.

Finished measurements
30 ½ (32 ½, 34 ½, 36 ½, 38 ½, 40 ½, 42 ½, 44 ½, 46 ½, 48 ½, 50 ½)" [77.5 (82.5, 87.5, 92.5, 98, 103, 108, 113, 118, 123, 128) cm] bust circumference, closed
Shown in 34 ¼" [87.5 cm] and 36 ½" [92.5 cm] with no ease.

Yarn
Chickadee by Quince & Co.
(100% American wool; 181 yd [166 m] / 50g)
• 5 (6, 6, 6, 7, 7, 8, 8, 9, 9, 9) skeins Twig 119 or Bird's Egg 106
 Or 905 (965, 1025, 1085, 1150, 1200, 1270, 1330, 1450, 1500, 1550) yd sport weight yarn.

Needles
• One 16" and 32" circular needle (circ) in size US 5 [3.75 mm]
• One set double-pointed needles (dpns) in size US 5 [3.75 mm] or one 40" circ if using magic loop to work sleeves
• One 32" circ in size US 4 [3.5 mm]
Or size to obtain gauge

Notions
• Stitch markers (m)
• Stitch holders or waste yarn
• Tapestry needle
• 8 (8, 8, 8, 8, 8, 8, 8, 10, 10, 10) ⁷⁄₈" buttons and matching thread

Gauge
24 sts and 36 rows = 4" in stockinette st with larger needles, after blocking.

Cardigan
Begin 1x1 rib
Using larger 32" circ and the long-tail cast on, CO 191 (203, 215, 227, 239, 251, 263, 275, 287, 299, 311) sts.
Row 1: (WS) P2, (k1, p1) to last st, p1.
Row 2: (RS) K2, (p1, k1) to last st, k1.
Repeat Rows 1 and 2 three times more, or until pc meas 1", ending on a RS row.

Next row *place markers*: (WS) Work in rib for 46 (49, 52, 55, 58, 61, 64, 67, 70, 73, 76) sts, pm for side, work in rib for 99 (105, 111, 117, 123, 129, 135, 141, 147, 153, 159) sts, pm for side, work in rib to end.
Row 1: (RS) Knit to first marker, sl m, k48 (51, 54, 57, 60, 63, 66, 69, 72, 75, 78) k2tog, knit to next marker, sl m, knit to end (1 st dec'd)—190 (202, 214, 226, 238, 250, 262, 274, 286, 298, 310) sts: 46 (49, 52, 55, 58, 61, 64, 67, 70, 73, 76) for each front and 98 (104, 110, 116, 122, 128, 134, 140, 146, 152, 158) for back.
Row 2: Purl.
Row 3 *dec row*: (RS) *Knit to 3 sts before marker, ssk, k1, sl m, k1, k2tog; rep from * once more, knit to end (4 st dec'd).
Continue in St st and repeat *dec row* every 8th row 6 times—162 (174, 186, 198, 210, 222, 234, 246, 258, 270, 282) sts.

Work even in St st for 13 (13, 13, 11, 13, 13, 11, 9, 13, 13, 11) rows, ending with a WS row.

Note: During the next section side increases will start to be worked **AND AT THE SAME TIME** you will begin working the Empire right and left front charts (p46-47) over the front sections of the cardigan. Each size begins working the chart on different rows. Please follow directions for your size.

Size 30 ½" only:
Next row *inc row*: (RS) Knit to 1 st before marker, M1R, k1, sl m, k1, M1L; rep from * once more, knit to end (4 sts inc'd).
Work 3 more rows in St st, then begin working from chart **AND AT THE SAME TIME** repeat *inc row* every 10th row once, then every 8th row 2 times more—178 sts.
Work even without increases until row 36 of chart is complete.

Sizes 32 ½, 38 ½, 46 ½" only:
Next row *inc row*: (RS) *Knit to 1 st before marker, M1R, k1, sl m, k1, M1L; rep from * once more, knit to end (4 sts inc'd).
Work 1 more row in St st, then begin working from chart on the next RS row **AND AT THE SAME TIME** repeat *inc row* every 10th (10th, 12th) row 1 (2, 2) times, then

every 8th (12th, 14th) row 2 (1, 1) times more—190 (226, 274) sts.
Work even without increases until row 38 (44, 54) of chart is complete.

Sizes 34 ¼, 40 ½, 48 ½" only:
Begin working from chart on the next RS row (which is also the first side increase row).
Next row *inc row*: (RS) *Knit to 1 st before marker, M1R, k1, sl m, k1, M1L; rep from * once more, knit to end (4 sts inc'd).
Continue working from chart and repeat *inc row* every 10th (10th, 12th) row 1 (2, 2) times, then every 8th (12th, 14th) row 2 (1, 1) more times—202 (238, 286) sts.
Work even without increases until row 40 (46, 56) of chart is complete.

Sizes 36 ½, 42 ½, 44 ½, 50 ½" only:
Begin working from chart on the next RS row and work 2 (2, 4, 2) rows.
Next row *inc row*: (RS) *Knit to 1 st before marker, M1R, k1, sl m, k1, M1L; rep from * once more, knit to end (4 sts inc'd).
Continue working from chart and repeat *inc row* every 10th (10th, 10th, 12th) row 1 (2, 2, 2) times, then every 8th (12th, 12th, 14th) row 2 (1, 1, 1) times more—214 (250, 262, 298) sts.
Work even without increases until row 42 (48, 50, 58) of chart is complete.

All sizes resume:
Divide back and fronts
Next row: (RS) Still working from chart, work to 4 (5, 6, 7, 7, 8, 8, 9, 9, 10, 11) sts before side marker, BO 8 (10, 12, 14, 14, 16, 16, 18, 18, 20, 22) sts (removing marker) work to 4 (5, 6, 7, 7, 8, 8, 9, 9, 10, 11) sts before next side marker, BO 8 (10, 12, 14, 14, 16, 16, 18, 18, 20, 22) sts, work to end of row—39 (41, 43, 45, 48, 50, 53, 55, 58, 60, 62) sts for each front and 84 (88, 92, 96, 102, 106, 112, 116, 122, 126, 130) sts for back. Piece meas 12 ½ (12 ½, 12 ½, 12 ½, 13 ¼, 13 ¼, 13 ¼, 13 ¼, 14 ¼, 14 ¼, 14 ¼)" [31.5 (31.5, 31.5, 31.5, 33.5, 33.5, 33.5, 33.5, 36, 36, 36) cm] from beg.

Place sts for right front and back onto holders or waste yarn.
Note: When working the fronts keep in pattern as established. Although the charts do not cover the remainder of the fronts, they can be used for reference.

Left front
Continue on sts of left front where yarn is still attached ready to start a WS row.
Note: Over the next 8 (8, 10, 10, 12, 12, 14, 14, 16, 16, 18) rows, keep the last 3 sts of WS rows in St st, working the rest in pattern as est.
Next row: (WS) Work in pattern as est.
Next row *dec row*: K1, ssk, work in pattern to end of row.

Continue working in pattern and repeat *dec row* every RS row 3 (3, 4, 4, 5, 5, 6, 6, 7, 7, 8) times more—35 (37, 38, 40, 42, 44, 46, 48, 50, 52, 53) sts remain. Continue working in pattern for another 23 (23, 21, 21, 19, 19, 17, 17, 15, 15, 13) rows, keeping 1 st at each end of row in St st and ending with a WS row. Front meas 5 ¾ (5 ¾, 6, 6, 6 ½, 6 ½, 7, 7, 7 ½, 7 ½, 7 ¾)" [14.5 (14.5, 15.25, 15.25, 16.5, 16.5, 17.75, 17.75, 19, 19, 19.75) cm] from underarm.

Shape left front neck
Next row: (RS) Work in pattern to last st, turn work.
Next row: (WS) Work bias bind off (see techniques) for 4 sts, work in pattern to end of row.
Repeat these two rows 3 times more.

Next row: (RS) Work in pattern to last st, turn work.
Next row: (WS) Work bias bind off for 3 sts, work in pattern to end of row.
Repeat these two rows 0 (0, 0, 0, 1, 1, 1, 2, 2, 3, 3) times more.

Sizes 36 ½, 40 ½, 42 ½, 46 ½" only:
Next row: (RS) Work in pattern to last st, turn work.
Next row: (WS) Work bias bind off for 2 sts, work in pattern to end of row.

All sizes resume:
16 (18, 19, 19, 20, 20, 22, 23, 23, 24, 25) sts remain.

After last bind off row, continue in pattern for another 16 (16, 20, 18, 22, 20, 24, 24, 26, 26, 30) rows, keeping 1 st at each end of row in St st.
Place sts on holder or waste yarn.

Right front
Re-attach yarn to sts of right front, ready to begin a WS row.
Note: Over the next 8 (8, 10, 10, 12, 12, 14, 14, 16, 16, 18) rows, keep the first 3 sts of WS rows in St st, working the rest in pattern as set.
Next row: (WS) Work in pattern as est.
Next row *dec row*: Work in pattern to last 3 sts of row, k2tog, k1 (1 st dec'd).
Continue working in pattern and repeat *dec row* every RS row 3 (3, 4, 4, 5, 5, 6, 6, 7, 7, 8) times more—35 (37, 38, 40, 42, 44, 46, 48, 50, 52, 53) sts remain. Continue working in pattern for another 22 (22, 20, 20, 18, 18, 16, 16, 14, 14, 12) rows, keeping 1 st at each end of row in St st and ending with a RS row. Front meas 5 ¾ (5 ¾, 6, 6, 6 ½, 6 ½, 7, 7, 7 ½, 7 ½, 7 ¾)" [14.5 (14.5, 15.25, 15.25, 16.5, 16.5, 17.75, 17.75, 19, 19, 19.75) cm] from underarm.

Shape right front neck
Next row: (WS) Work in pattern to last st, turn work.
Next row: (RS) Work bias bind off for 4 sts, work in pattern to end of row.
Repeat these two rows 3 times more.

Next row: (WS) Work in pattern to last st, turn work.
Next row: (RS) Work bias bind off for 3 sts, work in pattern to end of row.
Repeat these two rows 0 (0, 0, 0, 1, 1, 1, 2, 2, 3, 3) times more.

Sizes 36 ½, 40 ½, 42 ½, 46 ½" only:
Next row: (RS) Work in pattern to last st, turn work.
Next row: (WS) Work bias bind off for 2 sts, work in pattern to end of row.

All sizes resume:
16 (18, 19, 19, 20, 20, 22, 23, 23, 24, 25) sts remain.

After last bind off row, continue in pattern for another 17 (17, 21, 19, 23, 21, 25, 25, 27, 27, 31) rows, keeping 1 st at each end of row in St st.
Place sts on holder or waste yarn.

Back
Re-attach yarn to back sts, ready to start a WS row.
Purl 1 row.

Next row *dec row*: (RS) K1, ssk, knit to last 3 sts, k2tog, k1 (2 sts dec'd).
Continue in St st and repeat *dec row* every RS row 3 (3, 4, 4, 5, 5, 6, 6, 7, 7, 8) times more—76 (80, 82, 86, 90, 94, 98, 102, 106, 110, 112) sts remain.

Continue in St st for another 43 (43, 45, 45, 47, 47, 49, 49, 51, 51, 53) rows. Back meas 5 ¾ (5 ¾, 6, 6, 6 ½, 6 ½, 7, 7, 7 ½, 7 ½, 7 ¾)" [14.5 (14.5, 15.25, 15.25, 16.5, 16.5, 17.75, 17.75, 19, 19, 19.75) cm] from underarm. End with a WS row.

Shape back neck
Row 1: (RS) K18 (20, 21, 21, 22, 22, 24, 25, 25, 26, 27) sts, join new yarn and BO 40 (40, 40, 44, 46, 50, 50, 52, 56, 58, 58) sts at center back, knit to end.
Row 2: Working each side separately, purl across each shoulder.
Continue in St st and dec 1 st at each neck edge on the next 2 RS rows as follows: knit to 3 sts before neck edge, k2tog, k1; on other side, k1, ssk, knit to end.
Purl 1 row—16 (18, 19, 19, 20, 20, 22, 23, 23, 24, 25) sts remain for each shoulder.

Join shoulders

Place sts of right front shoulder on to the larger, shorter circ. Holding the right back shoulder sts and right front shoulder sts with right sides together, and using tail of yarn already in place, join sts of right front shoulder with right back shoulder using the three-needle bind off.

Repeat the shoulder join with the left front shoulder and left back shoulder sts.

Sleeves

Note: Sleeves are worked by picking up sts from the armhole and working short rows to shape the sleeve cap. The ratio for picking up sts around the armhole is about 1 out of every 2 rows.

Using the larger, shorter circ or dpns, and starting at the center of the bound off underarm sts, pick up and knit 4 (5, 6, 7, 7, 8, 8, 9, 9, 10, 11) bound off sts, then pick up and knit 29 (29, 31, 31, 33, 33, 35, 35, 37, 37, 39) sts to shoulder join, pm for shoulder seam, then pick up and knit 29 (29, 31, 31, 33, 33, 35, 35, 37, 37, 39) sts back down other side to underarm sts, pick up and knit 4 (5, 6, 7, 7, 8, 8, 9, 9, 10, 11) bound off underarm sts, pm for BOR—66 (68, 74, 76, 80, 82, 86, 88, 92, 94, 100) sts.

Shape sleeve cap

Note: See abbreviations for how to work w&t.
Short Row 1: (RS) Knit to 7 sts past shoulder seam marker, w&t.
Short Row 2: (WS) Purl to 7 sts past shoulder seam marker, w&t.
Short Row 3: Knit to wrapped st, work wrap with the st it wraps, w&t.
Short Row 4: Purl to wrapped st, work wrap with the st it wraps, w&t.
Repeat Short Rows 3–4 until all sts *except* the underarm sts have been worked.
After last w&t on a WS row, knit to m for BOR, picking up wrap as you come to it.
Knit 1 rnd and pick up the final wrap (as for a RS row).

Next rnd *dec rnd*: K1, k2tog, knit to 3 sts before end of rnd, ssk, k1(2 sts dec'd).
Continue in St st in the rnd and repeat *dec rnd* every 8th rnd 2 (2, 4, 4, 5, 5, 5, 5, 6, 10, 10) times more, then every 10th rnd 4 (4, 3, 3, 3, 3, 3, 3, 3, 0, 0) times more—52 (54, 58, 60, 62, 64, 68, 70, 72, 74, 78) sts remain.
Knit 16 (16, 12, 12, 8, 8, 8, 8, 6, 4, 4) rnds.
Next rnd: *K1, p1; rep from * around.
Repeat last rnd 8 times more.
BO all sts.

Button band

Note: Ratio for picking up sts for button bands is approx 3 out of 4 rows.
Using smaller circ, and beginning at neck edge of left front with RS facing, pick up and knit 107 (107, 107, 107, 113, 113, 113, 113, 117, 117, 117) sts down left front.

Row 1: (WS) *P1, k1; rep from * to last st, p1.
Row 2: (RS) *K1, p1; rep from * to last st, k1.
Rows 3–6: Repeat Rows 1–2 two times more.
BO all sts.

Buttonhole band

Using smaller circ, and beginning at hem edge of right front with RS facing, pick up and knit 107 (107, 107, 107, 113, 113, 113, 113, 117, 117, 117) sts up right front.
Row 1: (WS) *P1, k1; rep from * to last st, p1.
Row 2: (RS) *K1, p1; rep from * to last st, k1.
Row 3: Repeat Row 1.
Row 4 *buttonhole row:* [K1, p1] 2 (2, 2, 2, 3, 3, 3, 3, 2, 2, 2) times, k1, *yo, k2tog, [p1, k1] 6 (6, 6, 6, 6, 6, 6, 6, 5, 5, 5) times; repeat from * 6 (6, 6, 6, 6, 6, 6, 6, 8, 8, 8) times more, yo, k2tog, [p1, k1] 1(1, 1, 1, 2, 2, 2, 2, 1, 1, 1) times—8 (8, 8, 8, 8, 8, 8, 8, 10, 10, 10) buttonholes made.
Rows 5 and 6: Repeat Rows 1–2.
BO all sts.

Neckband

Note: Specific numbers for picking up sts around neck are given. However, the exact stitch count you end up with does not matter, as long as you use the right ratio for picking up sts for each section, which is described below.

Using smaller circ, and beginning at top of buttonhole band with RS facing, pick up and knit 6 sts across top of buttonhole band (1:1 ratio), then 19 (19, 19, 21, 22, 24, 24, 25, 27, 28, 28) sts across bound off neck sts (1:1 ratio), then 17 (17, 19, 18, 21, 19, 23, 23, 25, 25, 27) sts up right neck edge and down to bound off sts at back neck (3:4 ratio), then 40 (40, 40, 44, 46, 50, 50, 52, 56, 58, 58) sts across back neck (1:1 ratio), then 17 (17, 19, 18, 21, 19, 23, 23, 25, 25, 27) sts down to beginning of bound off neck sts for left front (3:4 ratio), then 19 (19, 19, 21, 22, 24, 24, 25, 27, 28, 28) sts across bound off neck sts (1:1 ratio), then 6 sts across top of left button band (1:1 ratio)—124 (124, 128, 134, 144, 148, 156, 160, 172, 176, 180) sts.
Cast on 2 sts, turn work to WS.
Work i-cord bind off as follows: *k2, ssk, slip 3 sts on right needle back to left needle and repeat from * until 3 sts remain, end sk2p. Cut yarn and pull tail through last loop.

Finishing

Weave in ends and block.
Attach buttons opposite buttonholes.

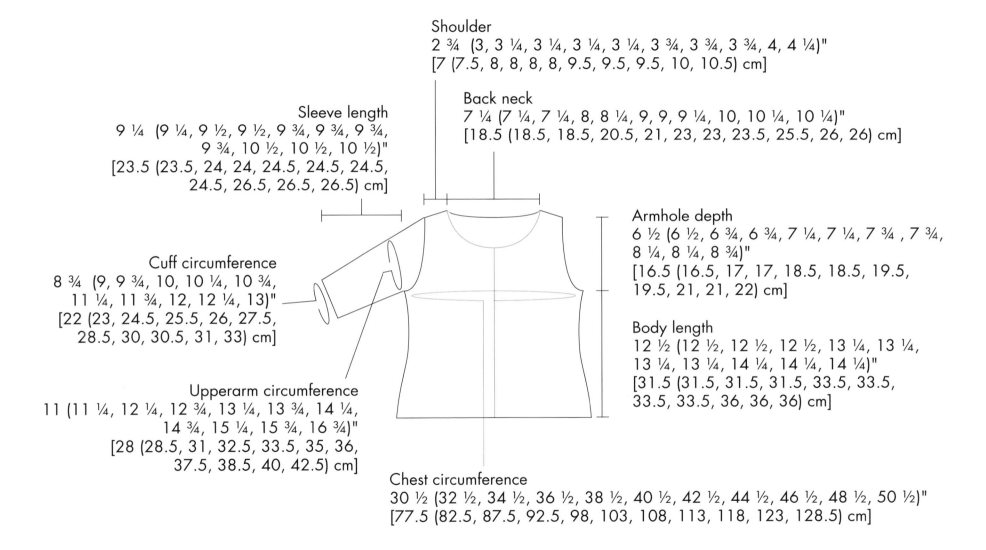

Shoulder
2 ¾ (3, 3 ¼, 3 ¼, 3 ¼, 3 ¼, 3 ¾, 3 ¾, 3 ¾, 4, 4 ¼)"
[7 (7.5, 8, 8, 8, 8, 9.5, 9.5, 9.5, 10, 10.5) cm]

Back neck
7 ¼ (7 ¼, 7 ¼, 8, 8 ¼, 9, 9, 9 ¼, 10, 10 ¼, 10 ¼)"
[18.5 (18.5, 18.5, 20.5, 21, 23, 23, 23.5, 25.5, 26, 26) cm]

Sleeve length
9 ¼ (9 ¼, 9 ½, 9 ½, 9 ¾, 9 ¾, 9 ¾,
9 ¾, 10 ½, 10 ½, 10 ½)"
[23.5 (23.5, 24, 24, 24.5, 24.5, 24.5,
24.5, 26.5, 26.5, 26.5) cm]

Armhole depth
6 ½ (6 ½, 6 ¾, 6 ¾, 7 ¼, 7 ¼, 7 ¾ , 7 ¾,
8 ¼, 8 ¼, 8 ¾)"
[16.5 (16.5, 17, 17, 18.5, 18.5, 19.5,
19.5, 21, 21, 22) cm]

Cuff circumference
8 ¾ (9, 9 ¾, 10, 10 ¼, 10 ¾,
11 ¼, 11 ¾, 12, 12 ¼, 13)"
[22 (23, 24.5, 25.5, 26, 27.5,
28.5, 30, 30.5, 31, 33) cm]

Body length
12 ½ (12 ½, 12 ½, 12 ½, 13 ¼, 13 ¼,
13 ¼, 13 ¼, 14 ¼, 14 ¼, 14 ¼)"
[31.5 (31.5, 31.5, 31.5, 33.5, 33.5,
33.5, 33.5, 36, 36, 36) cm]

Upperarm circumference
11 (11 ¼, 12 ¼, 12 ¾, 13 ¼, 13 ¾, 14 ¼,
14 ¾, 15 ¼, 15 ¾, 16 ¾)"
[28 (28.5, 31, 32.5, 33.5, 35, 36,
37.5, 38.5, 40, 42.5) cm]

Chest circumference
30 ½ (32 ½, 34 ½, 36 ½, 38 ½, 40 ½, 42 ½, 44 ½, 46 ½, 48 ½, 50 ½)"
[77.5 (82.5, 87.5, 92.5, 98, 103, 108, 113, 118, 123, 128.5) cm]

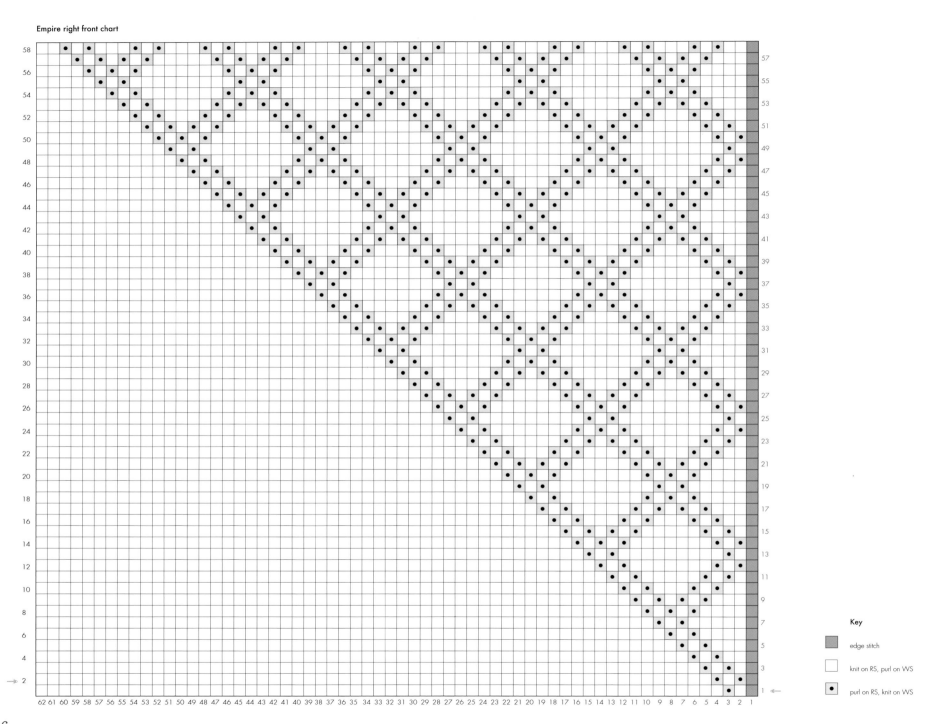

Key

edge stitch

knit on RS, purl on WS

• purl on RS, knit on WS

Empire left front chart

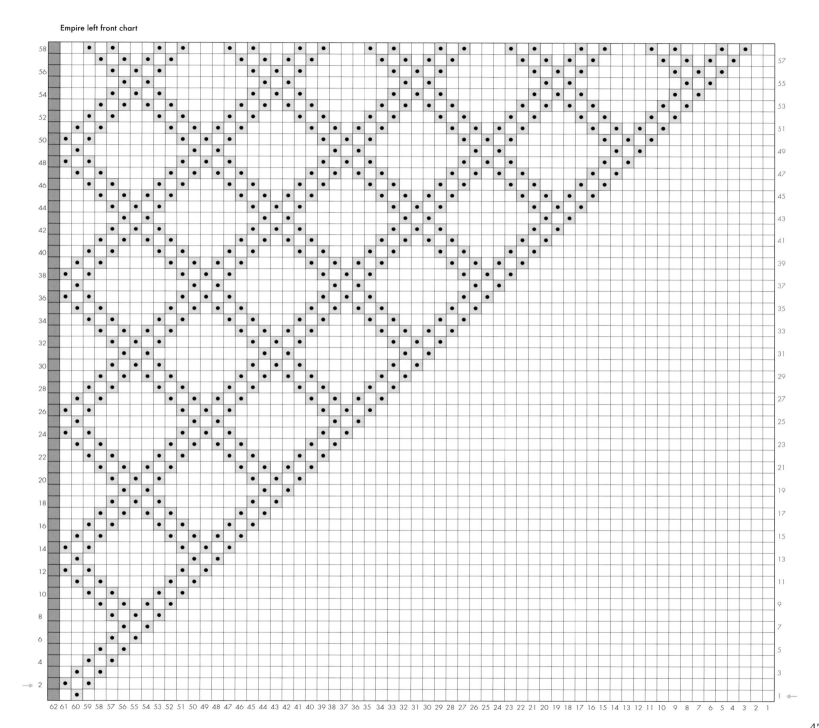

Ambrosia

This hooded, yoked cardigan is worked from the bottom up with sleeves and body joined at the underarm. The garter stitch band is picked up along the fronts and around the hood.

Finished measurements
27 (29 ½, 32 ¼, 35, 37 ½, 40 ¼, 43, 45 ½, 48 ¼, 51)" [68.5 (75, 82, 89, 95.5, 102, 109, 115.5, 122.5, 129.5)] cm bust circumference
Shown in 32 ¼" [82 cm] with 2 ¼" [5.75 cm] positive ease and 35" [95.5 cm] with 1" [2.5 cm] negative ease.

Yarn
Puffin by Quince & Co.
(100% American wool; 112 yd [102 m]/100 g)
- 7 (8, 8, 9, 10, 10, 11, 12, 12, 13) skeins Carrie's Yellow 125 (32 ¼") or Kittywake (35")
  Or 760 (830, 890, 985, 1050, 1115, 1200, 1275, 1340, 1420) yd chunky weight yarn.

Needles
- One 40" circular needle (circ) in size US 11 [8mm]
- One set double-pointed needles (dpns) in size US 11 [8mm] or use 40" circ to work magic loop for sleeves
- One 40" circ in size US 10 ½ [6.5mm]
- Cable needle (optional)

Or size to obtain gauge

Notions
- Stitch markers (m)
- Stitch holders or waste yarn
- Four 4" strips of contrasting color yarn in a similar weight to working yarn
- Tapestry needle for weaving in ends
- 3 toggle buttons 2 ¼" long

Gauge
12 sts and 17 rows= 4" [10 cm] in stockinette st with larger needles, after blocking.
11 sts and 24 rows= 4" [10 cm] in garter st with larger needles, after blocking.
11 sts and 22 rows= 4" [10 cm] in floating hexagon pattern with larger needles, after blocking.

Floating hexagon pattern (multiple of 6 sts +2)
Note: When working rows 6 and 18 you will be dropping sts from the needle. Although it is unlikely that the sts will unravel, try to keep movement of needles to a minimum at this point. You can of course use a cable needle to hold the dropped sts if you prefer.
Row 1: (WS) K3, *p2 BUT WRAP YARN TWICE FOR EACH PURL ST, k4; rep from * to last 5 sts, p2 BUT WRAP YARN TWICE FOR EACH PURL ST, k3.
Row 2: (RS) K3, *sl 2 wyib and drop extra wraps off needle, k4; rep from * to last

5 sts, sl 2 wyib and drop extra wraps off needle, k3.
Rows 3 and 5: K3, *sl 2 wyif, k4; rep from * to last 5 sts, sl 2 wyif, k3.
Row 4: K3, *sl 2 wyib, k4; rep from * to last 5 sts, sl 2 wyib, k3.
Row 6: K1, *sl 2 wyib, drop next st to front of work, sl the same 2 sts back onto the LH needle, pick up the dropped st and knit it, k2, drop next st to front of work, k2, pick up dropped st and knit it; rep from * to last st, k1.
Row 7: K1, *p1 BUT WRAP YARN TWICE, k4, p1 BUT WRAP YARN TWICE; rep from * to last st, k1.
Row 8: K1, *sl 1 wyib and drop extra wrap off needle, k4, sl 1 wyib and drop extra wrap off needle; rep from * to last st, k1.
Rows 9 and 11: K1, *sl 1 wyif, k4, sl 1 wyif; rep from * to last st, k1.
Row 10: K1, *sl 1 wyib, k4, sl 1 wyib; rep from * to last st, k1.
Row 12: Knit
Rows 13–17: Repeat rows 7–11.
Row 18: K1, *drop next st to front of work, k2, pick up dropped st and knit it, sl 2 wyib, drop next st to front of work, sl the same 2 sts back onto the LH needle, pick up the dropped st and knit it, k2; rep from * to last st, k1.
Rows 19–23: Repeat Rows 1–5.
Row 24: Knit.

Cardigan
Begin at hem
Using larger circ and the long-tail cast on, CO 92 (100, 108, 116, 124, 132, 140, 148, 156, 164) sts.
Work in garter st for 13 rows, beginning and ending on a WS row.

Next row *place markers*: (RS) K22 (24, 26, 28, 30, 32, 34, 36, 38, 40), pm, k48 (52, 56, 60, 64, 68, 72, 76, 80, 84), pm, knit to end (2 side markers placed).
Continue in St st for 13 rows.

Next row *dec row*: Knit to 3 sts before m, ssk, k1, sl m, k1, k2tog; rep from * once more, knit to end (4 sts dec'd).
Continue in St st and repeat *dec row* every 12th row 3 times more—76 (84, 92, 100, 108, 116, 124, 132, 140, 148) sts remain.

Work even in St st for 11 rows, ending with a WS row.
Place body sts on scrap yarn or spare needle. If you have yarn left, leave it attached to body and start a new ball for sleeves.

Sleeves
Using dpns or larger circ (for magic loop) and the long-tail cast on, CO 24 (26, 26, 28, 28, 30, 30, 34, 34, 36) sts. Pm for beg of rnd (BOR) and work in garter stitch in the rnd beg with a purl rnd, for 13 rnds (7 ridges).

Work even in St st for 30 (30, 30, 30, 28, 28, 20, 20, 14, 14) rnds.

Next rnd *inc rnd*: K1, k1-r/b, knit to last 2 sts, k1-r/b, k1 (2 sts inc'd).
Continue in St st and repeat *inc rnd* every 10th (10th, 10th, 10th, 8th, 8th, 8th, 8th, 8th, 8th) rnd 3 (3, 3, 3, 4, 4, 5, 5, 6, 6) times more—32 (34, 34, 36, 38, 40, 42, 46, 48, 50) sts total.

Continue in St st for 10 (10, 10, 10, 10, 10, 10, 10, 8, 8) more rnds.

Place first 2 (3, 3, 4, 4, 5, 5, 7, 8, 8) sts and last 2 (3, 3, 4, 4, 5, 5, 7, 8, 8) sts of rnd on stitch holder or waste yarn for underarm and place remaining 28 (28, 28, 28, 30, 30, 32, 32, 32, 34) sts on separate stitch holder or waste yarn.

Yoke
Pick up body and place on larger circ.

Join body and sleeves
Knit to 2 (3, 3, 4, 4, 5, 5, 7, 8, 8) sts before m, place next 4 (6, 6, 8, 8, 10, 10, 14, 16, 16) sts of body on stitch holder or waste yarn for underarm (remove m), knit across held sts of one sleeve, knit across sts of back to 2 (3, 3, 4, 4, 5, 5, 7, 8, 8) sts before next m, place next 4 (6, 6, 8, 8, 10, 10, 14, 16, 16) sts of body on stitch holder or waste yarn for underarm (remove m), knit across held sts of one sleeve, knit across remaining body sts to end—124 (128, 136, 140, 152, 156, 168, 168, 172, 184) sts on needles.

Next row: Purl.
Next row: Knit **AND AT SAME TIME** for sizes 27 (-, 32 ¼, -, -, 40 ¼, 43, 45 ½, 48 ¼, 51)", dec 2 (-, 2, -, -, 4, 4, 4, 2, 2) sts evenly across row—122 (128, 134, 140, 152, 152, 164, 164, 170, 182) sts.

Work Rows 1–24 of floating hexagon pattern once, then Rows 1–3 once more.

Next row *dec row*: K1, *sl 2 wyib, drop next st to front of work, sl same 2 sts back to LH needle, pick up dropped st and knit it, k2tog, drop next st off needle to front of work, k2, pick up dropped st and knit it; rep from * to last st, k1 [20 (21, 22, 23, 25, 25, 27, 27, 28, 30) sts dec'd]—102 (107, 112, 117, 127, 127, 137, 137, 142, 152) sts remain.
Work 1 (1, 1, 1, 1, 1, 3, 3, 3, 3) rows in St st.

Next row *dec row*: K3, *k3, k2tog; rep from * to last 4 sts, k4 [19 (20, 21, 22, 24, 24, 26, 26, 27, 29) sts dec'd]—83 (87, 91, 95, 103, 103, 111, 111, 115, 123) sts remain.
Work 1 (1, 3, 3, 3, 3, 3, 3, 3, 3) rows in St st.

Next row *dec row*: K3, *k2, k2tog; rep from * to last 4 sts, k4 [19 (20, 21, 22, 24, 24, 26, 26, 27, 29) sts dec'd]—64 (67, 70, 73, 79, 79, 85, 85, 88, 94) sts remain.

Work 1 (1, 1, 1, 3, 3, 3, 3, 5, 5) rows in St st.

Next row *dec row*: K3, *k1, k2tog; rep from *to last 4 sts, k4 [19 (20, 21, 22, 24, 24, 26, 26, 27, 29) sts dec'd]—45 (47, 49, 51, 55, 55, 59, 59, 61, 65) sts remain.

Short rows to shape back neck
Short Row 1: P35 (37, 39, 41, 45, 45, 49, 49, 51, 55), turn work, place one strip of contrast yarn across working yarn as for a Sunday Short Row (see techniques).
Short Row 2: K25 (27, 29, 31, 35, 35, 39, 39, 41, 45), turn work, place one strip of contrast yarn across working yarn as for a Sunday Short Row.
Short Row 3: P20 (22, 24, 26, 30, 30, 34, 34, 36, 40), turn work, place one strip of contrast yarn across working yarn as for a Sunday Short Row.
Short Row 4: K15 (17, 19, 21, 25, 25, 29, 29, 31, 35), turn work, place one strip of contrast yarn across working yarn as for a Sunday Short Row.
Next Row: Purl to end and resolve short rows as for a WS row.
Next Row: Knit and resolve short rows as for a RS row AND AT THE SAME TIME dec 1 (1, 1, 1, 3, 3, 5, 5, 5, 7) sts by working k2togs as evenly spaced across row—44 (46, 48, 50, 52, 52, 54, 54, 56, 58) sts remain.
BO all sts.

Begin hood
Using smaller circ and with RS facing, re-join yarn and pick up and knit 44 (46, 48, 50, 52, 52, 54, 54, 56, 58) sts across bound off neck sts.
Change to larger circ and work in St st until hood measures approx 11" [28 cm].

Short Rows to shape top of hood
Short Row 1: K18 (18, 20, 20, 20, 20, 22, 22, 22, 22) place one strip of contrast yarn across working yarn as for a Sunday Short Row, turn work and purl to end.
Short Row 2: K14 (14, 16, 16, 16, 16, 18, 18, 18, 18) place one strip of contrast yarn across working yarn as for a Sunday Short Row, turn work and purl to end.
Short Row 3: K10 (10, 12, 12, 12, 12, 14, 14, 14, 14) place one strip of contrast yarn across working yarn as for a Sunday Short Row, turn work and purl to end.

Knit one row, and resolve short rows as for a RS row.

Short Row 4: P18 (18, 20, 20, 20, 20, 22, 22, 22, 22), work a Sunday wrap, turn work and knit to end.
Short Row 5: P14 (14, 16, 16, 16, 16, 18, 18, 18, 18), work a Sunday wrap, turn work and knit to end.

Short Row 6: P10 (10, 12, 12, 12, 12, 14, 14, 14, 14), work a Sunday wrap, turn work and knit to end.

Purl one row, and resolve short rows as for a WS row.

Divide sts of hood in half onto two needles. Hold with right sides together, using a third needle work a three-needle bind off (see techniques).

Front Bands
Using waste yarn in a contrast color, mark placement for three buttonholes on right front. Place one at bottom of hexagon pattern, one in middle and one near to top.
Using smaller circ and starting at bottom of right front with RS facing, re-join yarn and pick up and knit along right front, hood, and left front edge, at a rate of 2 out of every 3 rows. The exact number of sts picked up doesn't matter.
Change to larger circ and work in garter st for 5 rows, ending with a WS row.
Buttonhole row: *Knit to buttonhole marker, yo, k2tog; rep from * twice more, knit to end.
Work 4 more rows in garter st, ending with a RS row.
BO all sts.

Finishing
Graft underarms together. Weave in ends. Block garment.
Sew on toggles opposite buttonholes.

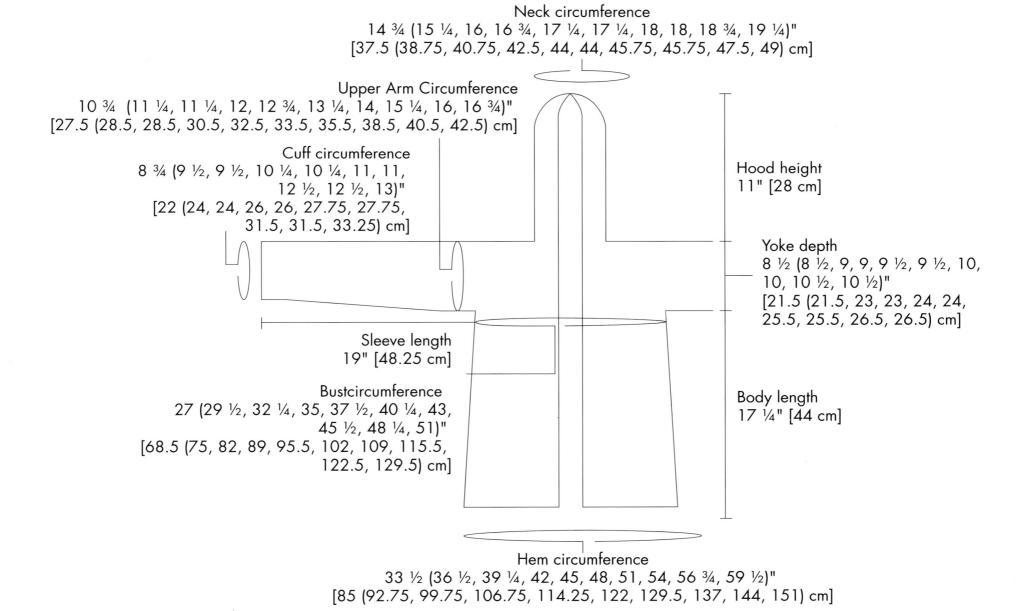

Neck circumference
14 ¾ (15 ¼, 16, 16 ¾, 17 ¼, 17 ¼, 18, 18, 18 ¾, 19 ¼)"
[37.5 (38.75, 40.75, 42.5, 44, 44, 45.75, 45.75, 47.5, 49) cm]

Upper Arm Circumference
10 ¾ (11 ¼, 11 ¼, 12, 12 ¾, 13 ¼, 14, 15 ¼, 16, 16 ¾)"
[27.5 (28.5, 28.5, 30.5, 32.5, 33.5, 35.5, 38.5, 40.5, 42.5) cm]

Cuff circumference
8 ¾ (9 ½, 9 ½, 10 ¼, 10 ¼, 11, 11,
12 ½, 12 ½, 13)"
[22 (24, 24, 26, 26, 27.75, 27.75,
31.5, 31.5, 33.25) cm]

Hood height
11" [28 cm]

Yoke depth
8 ½ (8 ½, 9, 9, 9 ½, 9 ½, 10,
10, 10 ½, 10 ½)"
[21.5 (21.5, 23, 23, 24, 24,
25.5, 25.5, 26.5, 26.5) cm]

Sleeve length
19" [48.25 cm]

Bustcircumference
27 (29 ½, 32 ¼, 35, 37 ½, 40 ¼, 43,
45 ½, 48 ¼, 51)"
[68.5 (75, 82, 89, 95.5, 102, 109, 115.5,
122.5, 129.5) cm]

Body length
17 ¼" [44 cm]

Hem circumference
33 ½ (36 ½, 39 ¼, 42, 45, 48, 51, 54, 56 ¾, 59 ½)"
[85 (92.75, 99.75, 106.75, 114.25, 122, 129.5, 137, 144, 151) cm]

the accessories

Rubens

Hampshire

Porter

Honey Crisp

Cortland

Rubens

Welted pattern

Rnd 1: With smaller circ, purl.
Rnd 2: Knit.
Rnd 3: Purl.
Change to larger circ.
Rnds 4–5: Knit.
Change back to smaller circ.
Rnd 6: Knit.
Rnd 7: Purl.
Rnd 8: Knit.
Rnd 9: Purl.
Repeat Rnds 4–9 for welted pattern.

Hat

With smaller circ and the long-tail cast on, CO 100 sts.
Pm and join for working in the rnd.
Work Rnds 1–9 of welted pattern.
Repeat Rnds 4–9 once more, then Rnds 4–7 once more. (Remember to continue changing needle sizes.)
Next rnd *inc rnd:* *K4, k1-f/b; rep from * around (20 sts inc'd)—120 sts total.
Next rnd: Purl.
Repeat Rnds 4–9 ten times more, then rnds 4–7 once more; pc meas approx 9" [23 cm] from beg.

Shape crown

Change to dpns, or 40" circ if using magic loop, as necessary.
Rnd 1 *dec rnd:* *K2, k2tog; rep from * around (30 sts dec'd)—90 sts rem.
Rnd 2: Purl.
Rnd 3 *dec rnd:* *K1, k2tog; rep from * around (30 sts dec'd)—60 sts rem.
Rnd 4: Purl.
Rnd 5 *dec rnd:* *K2tog; rep from * around (30 sts dec'd)—30 sts rem.
Rnd 6: Purl.
Rnd 7: Rep Rnd 5 (15 sts dec'd)—15 sts rem.
Cut yarn leaving a tail and draw through remaining loops. Secure to the WS of the hat.

Finishing

Weave in ends. Block hat by giving it a soak in a gentle wool wash.

Hampshire

Finished measurements
17" [43.25 cm] brim circumference and 9 ½" [24 cm] brim to crown

Yarn
Chickadee by Quince & Co.
(100% American wool; 181 yd [166 m] / 50g)
- 2 skeins in Kumlien's Gull 152
  Or 240 yd sport weight yarn.

Needles
- One 16" circular needle (circ) in size US 5 [3.75 mm]
- One set double-pointed needles (dpns) in size US 5 [3.75 mm] or one 40" circ if using magic loop
- One 16" circular needle (circ) in size US 10 [6 mm]
- One set double-pointed needles (dpns) in size US 10 [6 mm] or one 40" circ if using magic loop

Or size to obtain gauge

Notions
- Stitch marker (m)
- Tapestry needle

Gauge
24 sts and 37 rnds = 4" [10 cm] in welted pattern, after blocking.

Gauge

11 sts and 28 rnds = 4" [10 cm] in slipped stitch mesh pattern, after blocking.

Slipped stitch mesh pattern (multiple of 2 sts)

Rnd 1: Knit.
Rnd 2: *Sl1 wyif, p1; rep from * around.
Rnd 3: *Sl1 wyif, k1; rep from * around.
Rnd 4: Bring yarn to front of work, *yo, p2tog; rep from * around.
Rnd 5: Purl.
Rnd 6: Knit.
Rep Rnds 1–6 for slipped stitch mesh pattern.

Hat

Using circ and the long-tail cast on, CO 56 sts. Pm and join to begin working in the rnd.
Note: When instructed to slip sts in the pattern, slip purlwise.
Setup rnd: *K2, p2; rep from * around.
Work in K2, p2 rib as est for 8 (12) total rnds.

Next rnd *inc rnd:* *K1, k1-r/b, k2; rep from * around (14 sts inc'd)—70 sts total.

Begin hat body

Work Rnds 1–6 of slipped stitch mesh pattern a total of 4 (6) times.

Shape crown

Change to dpns or 40" circ for magic loop as necessary.
Rnd 1 *dec rnd:* *K1, k2tog, k2, k2tog; rep from * around (20 sts dec'd)—50 sts rem.
Rnd 2: *Sl1 wyif, p1; rep from * around.
Rnd 3: *Sl1 wyif, k1; rep from * around.
Rnd 4: Bring yarn to front of work, *yo, p2tog; rep from * around.
Rnd 5: Purl.
Rnd 6: Knit.
Rnd 7 *dec rnd:* *K1, k2tog, k2tog; rep from * around (20 sts dec'd)—30 sts rem.
Rnd 8: *Sl1 wyif, p1; rep from * around.
Rnd 9: *Sl1 wyif, k1; rep from * around.
Rnd 10: Bring yarn to front of work, *yo, p2tog; rep from * around.
Rnd 11: Purl.
Rnd 12 *dec rnd:* *K1, k2tog; rep from * around (10 sts dec'd)—20 sts rem.
Rnd 13 *dec rnd:* *K2tog; rep from * around (10 sts dec'd)—10 sts rem.
Cut yarn and draw through remaining sts.

Rubens

Finished measurements

8" [20.25 cm] brim circumference and 7 (9)" [17.75 (22.75) cm] brim to crown

Yarn

Puffin by Quince & Co.
(100% American wool; 112 yd [102 m] / 100 g)
- 1 skein Carrie's Yellow 125 (slouchy version) or Bird's Egg 106 (Shorter pom pom version)
  Or 90 (112) yd chunky weight yarn.
  Note: The slouchy version of this hat uses almost the entire skein. If you are concerned about running out of yarn it might be better to get an extra skein just in case.

Needles

- One 16" circular needle (circ) in size US 10 [6 mm]
- One set of double-pointed needles (dpns) in size US 10 [6 mm] or 40" circ if using magic loop method

Or size to obtain gauge

Notions

- Stitch marker (m)
- Tapestry needle for weaving in ends
- 4" wide piece of cardboard for making pompom (optional)

Finishing

Weave in ends. If you do this as invisibly as possible then you will have a reversible hat if working the slouchy version.

Soak hat in a gentle wool wash for 20 minutes. Then block, stretching out the lacey/holey part for extra slouch but not the ribbing!

Pom Pom: Cut a 4" wide piece of sturdy cardboard and wrap yarn all the way around approx 40 times. Cut yarn and carefully slide wraps off the cardboard. Take a separate piece of yarn and tie securely around the center of the wrapped yarn. Cut both ends of the wraps and attach the pom pom to the hat, trimming it as needed.

Porter

Finished measurements
66" [167.5 cm] in length, 6" [15.25 cm] wide, slightly stretched

Yarn
Puffin by Quince & Co.
(100% American wool; 112 yd [102 m] / 100 g)
- 3 skeins in Lupine 116 (240g)
  Or 295 yd chunky weight yarn.

Needles
- One pair in size US 11 [8 mm]

Or size to obtain gauge

Notions
- Tapestry needle for weaving in ends
- Crochet hook in comparable size to needles to create fringe

Gauge
15 sts and 18 rows = 4" in rib pattern, slightly stretched, after blocking.

Scarf
Using long-tail cast on, CO 23 sts.

Begin rib pattern
Row 1: *K2, p2; rep from * to last 3 sts, k2, p1.
Repeat Row 1 until scarf meas 66" [167.5 cm] from beg.
BO all sts in pattern.

Finishing
Weave in ends. Block scarf by soaking in a gentle wool wash.
Cut lengths of yarn for fringe. Fold two lengths of yarn in half and pull through the CO and BO edges of the scarf using a crochet hook to create a loop. Pull the ends of the fringe through the loop to secure to the scarf. Space as desired along each edge.

Honey Crisp

Finished measurements
70 ½" [179 cm] in circumference, 4 ¼" [10.75 cm] tall

Yarn
Puffin by Quince & Co.
(100% American wool; 112 yd [102 m] / 100 g)
• 2 skeins in Clay 113
  Or 220 yd chunky weight yarn.

Needles
• One 40" circular needle (circ) in size US 11 [8 mm]
Or size to obtain gauge

Notions
• Stitch marker (m)
• Tapestry needle

Gauge
10 sts and 28 rnds = 4" [10 cm] in slipped stitch mesh pattern, after blocking.

Slipped stitch mesh pattern (multiple of 2 sts)
Rnd 1: Purl.
Rnds 2–3: Knit.
Rnd 4: *Sl1 wyif, p1; rep from * around.
Rnd 5: *Sl1 wyif, k1; rep from * around.
Rnd 6: Bring yarn to front of work, *yo, p2tog; rep from * around.
Rep Rnds 1–6 for slipped stitch mesh pattern.

Cowl
Using the long-tail cast on, CO 180 sts.
Pm and join to begin working in the rnd.
Work Rnds 1–6 of slipped stitch mesh pattern.
Repeat Rnds 1–6 three times more.
Repeat Rnds 1–3 once more.
Next rnd: Purl.
BO all sts loosely.

Finishing
Weave in ends and wet block to measurements.

Stitch pattern (multiple of 2 sts)
Rnd 1: Knit.
Rnd 2: *Sl1 purlwise wyib, k1, yo, pass the slipped st over the knitted stitch and yarn over; rep from * around.
Rep Rnds 1–2 for stitch pattern.

Leg warmers (make 2)
Using smaller needles and the long-tail cast on, CO 60 sts.
Pm and join to begin working in the rnd.
Setup rnd: *K1, p1; rep from * around.
Work in k1, p1 rib as est until pc meas approx 1 ¼" [3.25 cm].
Change to larger needles.

Work Rnds 1–2 of stitch pattern until pc meas approx 13" [33.5 cm] from beg.

Change back to smaller needles.
Work in k1, p1 rib for ¾" [2 cm].
BO all sts in rib.

Finishing
Weave in ends using tapestry needle.
Block leg warmers by soaking in a gentle wool wash.

Cortland

Finished measurements
11" [28 cm] in circumference and 13 ¾" [35.5 cm] in length
Yarn
Lark by Quince & Co.
(100 % American wool; 134 yd [123 m] / 50 g)
- 3 skeins Pomegranate 112
  Or 330 yd worsted weight yarn.
Needles
- One set double-pointed needles (dpns) in size US 7 [4.5 mm] or one 40" circular needle (circ) if using magic loop method
- One set double-pointed needles (dpns) in size US 8 [5 mm] or one 40" circ if using magic loop method
Or size to obtain gauge
Notions
- Stitch marker (m)
- Tapestry needle
Gauge
22 sts and 30 rnds = 4" [10 cm] in stitch pattern, after blocking.

the beginner sweater

Granny Smith

This pattern is intended for those who are new to sweater knitting. It's a simple top down raglan style sweater with easy yarn over increases and a little bit of shaping in the body and sleeves. Some extra notes and reminders are included in this pattern to help keep you on track. However, it is recommended that you have a good knitting reference book handy to give further explanations.

The first decision to make when knitting a sweater is what size to pick. Really, this comes down to what sort of ease you want your sweater to have. If you want it to be fitted, you need to choose a size smaller or close to your actual chest measurement; if you like a looser look, pick a size that is greater than your chest measurement. If you're not sure, then perhaps find a sweater in your closet that you like the fit of and measure it.

If you are new to reading sweater patterns you may find all the information a little overwhelming to begin with. The best approach is just to start at the beginning and have faith that you'll be able to figure things out as you go along. It worked for me when I first started knitting!

Some things that might be helpful:
• All abbreviations in a pattern should be listed somewhere. If there aren't too many, then you'll soon remember what they mean. If there is an unusual technique, often this will be described in detail under a techniques section.
• When you've decided what size to make, it might be helpful to go through the pattern and highlight all the numbers that pertain to your size. The sizes are listed with smallest first, and the rest in ascending order in parentheses. This corresponds to any point in your pattern where there is a number followed by several more in parentheses.
• Make any kind of notes you need to on your pattern as you go along, and always mark where you last stopped. Row counters can be helpful to keep track of where you are, too.
• Most garment patterns are going to begin with listing things like the sizes offered, materials needed, yardage requirements, gauge, and sometimes some information about the construction of the garment. Make sure you have all the required needles, yarn, tools, etc.
• Most importantly, make sure you do a gauge swatch! Getting the correct gauge is crucial to ending up with a sweater that will fit you the way you want. Make sure your swatch is a good size (at least 4" by 4") and always wash and block it.
• Don't be scared to ask your local yarn store for help. Most stores offer drop-in knitting consultations and are happy to offer assistance. You can also email me!

So, take a deep breath and start knitting your first sweater!

Finished measurements

31 (33, 35 ½, 38 ½, 41 ½, 43 ¾, 46, 49, 52 ¼)" [78.75 (83.75, 90.25, 97.75, 105.5, 111, 117, 124.5, 132.75) cm] bust circumference
Shown in size 31" [78.75 cm] with 1" [2.5 cm] of positive ease.

Yarn

Osprey by Quince & Co.
(100% American wool; 170 yd [155 m] / 100 g)
• 4 (5, 5, 6, 6, 7, 7, 7, 8) skeins in Parsley 129
 Or 680 (750, 840, 905, 965, 1065, 1080, 1160, 1260) yd Aran weight yarn.

Needles

• One 16", 24", and 32" circular needle (circ) in size US 10 [6 mm]
• One set of double-pointed needles (dpns) in size US 10 [6 mm] or one 40" circular if using magic loop to work sleeves

Or size to obtain gauge

Notions

• Stitch markers (m)
• Stitch holders or waste yarn
• Tapestry needle for weaving in ends
• 1 ¾ yd of ribbon ⅜" wide

Gauge

15 sts and 22 rnds = 4" [10 cm] in stockinette stitch, after blocking.

Note

This sweater is knit in the round from the top down using raglan shaping. The raglan increases are formed by making yarnovers which create decorative holes along the raglan seams. The sleeves have a gentle bell shape finished with a simple garter stitch at the cuff. The little patch pocket is an optional addition.

Sweater
Begin at neck

Using the 16" circ and the long-tail cast on, CO 80 (80, 80, 80, 88, 88, 88, 96, 96) sts.
Place marker (pm) and join for knitting in the round.
Double check that you have the right number of stitches before beginning and make sure the stitches aren't twisted. If you have never knit in the round before then see this link for help: http://www.knittinghelp.com/videos/advanced-techniques.

Rnd 1: Purl.
Rnd 2: Knit.
If you want to omit the eyelet-ribbon part of the sweater, simply repeat Rnd 1 once more, then proceed to Rnd 6.

Sizes 31", 33", 35 ½", 38 ½" [78.75 (83.75, 90.25, 97.75) cm] only:

Rnd 3 *eyelet rnd*: *K3, yo, k2tog ; rep from * around. When asked to repeat an action from * all you have to do is go back to the * symbol and work through the same set of instructions.
Proceed to section marked All sizes resume.

Sizes 41 ½", 43 ¾", 46" [105.5, 111, 117 cm] only:

Rnd 3 *eyelet rnd*: *(K3, yo, k2tog, k4, yo, k2tog) ; rep from * around. When asked to repeat an action from * all you have to do is go back to the * symbol and work through the same set of instructions.
Proceed to section marked All sizes resume.

Sizes 49", 52 ¼" [124.5, 132.75 cm] only:

Rnd 3 *eyelet rnd*: *K4, yo, k2tog ; rep from * around. When asked to repeat an action from * all you have to do is go back to the * symbol and work through the same set of instructions.
Proceed to section marked All sizes resume.

All sizes resume:

Rnd 4: Knit.
Rnd 5: Purl.
When working the following set up rnd make sure your beginning of rnd marker is a different color than the ones you use for the raglan markers.
Rnd 6 *set up rnd*: K14 (14, 14, 15, 17, 17, 18, 20, 20), pm, k1, pm, k10 (10, 10, 8, 8, 8, 6, 6, 6), pm, k1, pm, k28 (28, 28, 30, 34, 34, 36, 40, 40), pm, k1, pm, k10 (10, 10, 8, 8, 8, 6, 6, 6), pm, k1, pm, k14 (14, 14, 15, 17, 17, 18, 20, 20).
Rnd 7 *inc rnd*: *Knit to m, yo, sl m, k1, sl m, yo; rep from * three times more, knit to end.
You have increased 8 sts—88 (88, 88, 88, 96, 96, 96, 104, 104) sts total.
The raglan shaping is formed by making yarnovers on either side of a central stitch. As you continue with the raglan shaping, make sure that on the central stitch is always lining up with the one above it. Sometimes the markers may slip to the wrong side of the yarn over.
Rnd 8: Knit all sts and slip markers as you come to them.
When you come to the yarn over stitches from the previous row, simply knit them.

Repeat the last two rnds 12 (14, 16, 18, 18, 20, 20, 21, 23) times more—184 (200, 216, 232, 240, 256, 256, 272, 288) sts total after all rnds completed.
Change to longer circular needles as necessary.

As you gain more stitches, it will be more comfortable to use one of the longer circular needles.

Something you could do once all increase rnds have been worked is to slip all the stitches onto a long piece of waste yarn (just thread a tapestry needle with the yarn and slip stitches onto it—making sure to slip the stitches purlwise). Then try your sweater on by placing it over your head. Make sure that the raglan seam comes at least an inch below your armpit. If it doesn't then you may want to knit some plain rows to add a bit more length.

Divide body and sleeves

Now you are going to place the sleeve stitches on waste yarn while you continue to work the body only.

Next rnd: K27 (29, 31, 34, 36, 38, 39, 42, 44), remove marker and place next 38 (42, 46, 48, 48, 52, 50, 52, 56) sts on waste yarn for sleeves, removing other markers as you come to them (thread a tapestry needle with a piece of contrasting color yarn that is long enough to hold all the sleeve stitches then simply slip the stitches onto the tapestry needle, slipping them purlwise), CO 2 (2, 2, 2, 3, 3, 4, 4, 5) sts using the backward loop cast on (see techniques), pm, CO 2 (2, 2, 2, 3, 3, 4, 4, 5) more sts using the backward loop cast on, knit across 54 (58, 62, 68, 72, 76, 78, 84, 88) sts to next marker, remove marker and place next 38 (42, 46, 48, 48, 52, 50, 52, 56) sts on waste yarn for sleeves as before, CO 2 (2, 2, 2, 3, 3, 4, 4, 5) sts, pm, CO 2 (2, 2, 2, 3, 3, 4, 4, 5) more sts, knit to end—116 (124, 132, 144, 156, 164, 172, 184, 196) sts total.

You are now working on the body stitches only and have placed 2 side seam markers. You will be decreasing some stitches at the side seams as you head towards the waist of the sweater then increasing stitches again as you head towards the hips.

Continue on sts of body only.

Knit 8 (8, 8, 8, 8, 6, 6, 6, 6) rnds.

Next rnd *dec rnd*: *Knit to 3 sts before marker, ssk, k1, sl m, k1, k2tog; rep from * once more, knit to end of rnd (4 sts dec'd).

Continue in St st in the rnd (this just means you knit every rnd) and repeat *dec rnd* every 9th (9th, 11th, 11th, 11th, 8th, 8th, 8th, 8th) rnd 2 (2, 2, 2, 2, 3, 3, 3, 3) more times.

You now have 104 (112, 120, 132, 144, 148, 156, 168, 180) sts.

Work even in St st in the rnd for 8 (8, 8, 8, 8, 6, 6, 6, 6) rnds.

Next rnd *inc rnd*: *Knit to 1 st before m, M1R, k1, sl m, k1, M1L; rep from * once more (4 sts inc'd).

Continue in St st and repeat *inc rnd* every 7th rnd 2 (2, 2, 2, 2, 3, 3, 3, 3) times more—116 (124, 132, 144, 156, 164, 172, 184, 196) sts total.

Work even in St st for 7 rnds.

Next rnd: Purl.
Next rnd: Knit.
Repeat last two rnds six times more.
Next rnd: Purl.
Bind off all sts.

Sleeves

Note: When knitting a smaller circumference in the round, double pointed needles (dpns) are often used. The stitches are divided up between 3 dpns, and then a 4th is used to knit across them. Another method which can be used to knit small circumferences is the magic loop method. This requires using a circular needle with a long cable. In this case the sts being worked are divided in half with a loop of cable coming out both ends. Tutorials for either of these methods can be found at http://www.knittinghelp.com/videos/advanced-techniques.

Using dpns or long circ (if using the magic loop method) and starting at the center of the stitches that were cast on for the underarm, pick up and knit 2 (2, 2, 2, 3, 3, 4, 4, 5) sts (see techniques for how to pick up stitches), then place 38 (42, 46, 48, 48, 52, 50, 52, 56) held sts of sleeves onto needles and knit across them, pick up and knit 2 (2, 2, 2, 3, 3, 4, 4, 5) sts from the underarm sts, pm for BOR.

You have 42 (46, 50, 52, 54, 58, 58, 60, 66) sts total.

Knit 5 rnds.

Next rnd *dec rnd*: K1, k2tog, knit to last 3 sts, ssk, k1 (2 sts dec'd).

Continue in St st in the rnd and repeat *dec rnd* every 9th (9th, 9th, 9th, 9th, 7th, 7th, 7th, 5th) rnd 3 (3, 4, 4, 4, 5, 5, 5, 7) times more—34 (38, 40, 42, 44, 46, 46, 48, 50) sts remain.

Continue in St st in the rnd for 40 (40, 31, 31, 31, 30, 30, 30, 30) rnds more. Sleeve meas approx 13 ½ (13 ½, 13 ½, 13 ½, 13 ½, 13, 13, 13, 13)" [34.25 (34.25, 34.25, 34.25, 34.25, 33, 33, 33, 33) cm] from underarm.

Next rnd *inc rnd*: K1, M1L, knit to 1 st before end of rnd, M1R, k1 (2 sts inc'd).

Continue in St st and repeat *inc rnd* every 5th rnd twice more—40 (44, 46, 48, 50, 52, 52, 54, 56) sts total.

Next rnd: Purl.
Next rnd: Knit.
Repeat last 2 rnds six times more.

Next rnd: Purl.
Bind off all sts.

Pocket (optional)

Note: Although the pocket is easy to knit, seaming it on to the actual sweater can be a little tricky. Make sure to look up tutorials on how to seam before you begin and go slowly. See tutorial here: http://www.vogueknitting.com/pattern_help/how-to/beyond_the_basics/pockets.aspx

With shorter circ, CO 16 sts.
Knit 5 rows.
Next row: (RS) Knit
Next row: (WS) Purl
Repeat last two rows six times more.
Bind off all sts.

Finishing

Finishing is another important part of the whole process. Don't skip any of this! Yarn blooms and gets softer after it has been blocked so you will end up with a nicer looking and feeling sweater.
Weave in any ends of yarn and close any holes that may be showing at the underarm seams using a tapestry needle. Work from the wrong side of the work carrying the yarn in and out of the purl bumps for several stitches to secure them.
Seam pocket to sweater. Decide where you want to place it and then begin by seaming the bottom horizontal edge. Next, do each side of the pocket.
Block sweater by soaking it in a wool wash in cool water for 20 mins. Let the water drain out then very gently squeeze some more excess water from the sweater. Lift it very carefully in one big bundle onto a towel. Roll it up in the towel, squeezing more water out. Then lay it out on a separate clean and dry towel. Use a tape measure to check the measurements as you lay it out, being careful not to overstretch anything as you do so. Do not move sweater until it is completely dry.
When the sweater is dry, thread the piece of ribbon through the eyelet holes at the neckline and wear your sweater proudly!

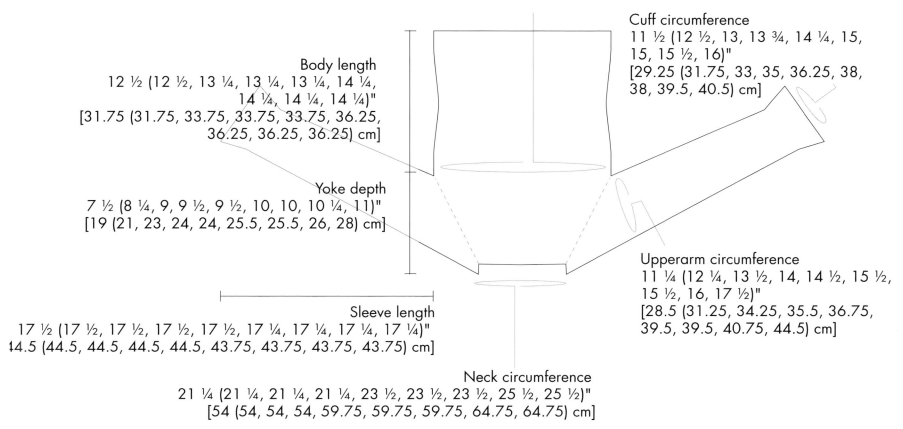

Bust circumference
31 (33, 35 ¼, 38 ½, 41 ½, 43 ¾, 46, 49, 52 ¼)"
[78.75 (83.75, 90.25, 97.75, 105.5, 111, 117, 124.5, 132.75) cm]

Cuff circumference
11 ½ (12 ½, 13, 13 ¾, 14 ¼, 15, 15, 15 ½, 16)"
[29.25 (31.75, 33, 35, 36.25, 38, 38, 39.5, 40.5) cm]

Body length
12 ½ (12 ½, 13 ¼, 13 ¼, 13 ¼, 14 ¼, 14 ¼, 14 ¼, 14 ¼)"
[31.75 (31.75, 33.75, 33.75, 33.75, 36.25, 36.25, 36.25, 36.25) cm]

Yoke depth
7 ½ (8 ¼, 9, 9 ½, 9 ½, 10, 10, 10 ¼, 11)"
[19 (21, 23, 24, 24, 25.5, 25.5, 26, 28) cm]

Upperarm circumference
11 ¼ (12 ¼, 13 ½, 14, 14 ½, 15 ½, 15 ½, 16, 17 ½)"
[28.5 (31.25, 34.25, 35.5, 36.75, 39.5, 39.5, 40.75, 44.5) cm]

Sleeve length
17 ½ (17 ½, 17 ½, 17 ½, 17 ½, 17 ¼, 17 ¼, 17 ¼, 17 ¼)"
44.5 (44.5, 44.5, 44.5, 44.5, 43.75, 43.75, 43.75, 43.75) cm]

Neck circumference
21 ¼ (21 ¼, 21 ¼, 21 ¼, 23 ½, 23 ½, 23 ½, 25 ½, 25 ½)"
[54 (54, 54, 54, 59.75, 59.75, 59.75, 64.75, 64.75) cm]

Techniques

Stockinette stitch (St st)
Flat
Knit on the RS and purl on the WS.
In the round
Knit every round.

Garter stitch
Flat
Knit every row.
In the rnd
Rnd 1: Knit.
Rnd 2: Purl.
Rep Rnds 1 and 2.

Long-tail cast on
Set Up: To work this cast on you will need a long tail of yarn. The general rule of thumb for determining how long to make the tail is to allow for approx ½ an inch of yarn per stitch to be cast on. A quick way to do this is to wrap the yarn around the needle 10 times (to approximate 10 stitches worth) take that length of yarn and multiply according to number of stitches you need to cast on (remembering that each length is worth 10 stitches). Once you have your tail make a slipknot and place onto the right hand needle. Put the thumb and index finger of your left hand in between the yarns hanging from the needle so that the working yarn goes around the index finger and the tail end around the thumb. Turn your left hand so that the palm faces up to make a V shape with the yarns. Keep the hanging ends of the yarn in place with your other fingers. See tutorial here: http://www.knittinghelp.com/video/play/long-tail-cast-on.

Step 1: Take the needle under and up through the loop on the thumb.
Step 2: Take the needle over the first strand on the index finger, then back down through the center of the loop on the thumb.
Step 3: Remove thumb from the yarns and tighten the stitch just formed.
Step 4: Replace thumb and index finger into yarn to form the V shape.
Repeat Steps 1–4 until desired number of stitches have been cast on.

German Twisted Cast On
(Or Old Norwegian Cast On)
A photo tutorial for this cast on can be found on my website www.theshetlandtrader.com under tutorials.
Set up as for long-tail cast on.

Step 1: Bring needle under both yarns that are around thumb.
Step 2: Bring needle down through the loop formed by the thumb.
Step 3: Take the needle back towards the index finger.
Step 4: Take the needle over the top of yarn coming from the index finger to catch it.
Step 5: Next bring the needle back down through the loop on the thumb.
Step 6: Drop loop off the thumb and tighten up the stitch just formed.

Sunday Short Rows
Have your strips of contrasting color yarn ready before beginning.
For RS and WS rows, work to the turning point, turn work and lay a strip of CC yarn across working yarn, then continue to work as normal, letting the CC yarn get caught up in the working yarn where it will act as a placeholder.

To resolve the gap on RS rows: Work to the turning point then pull on both ends of the CC yarn bringing up a loop. Insert the LH needle into this loop and knit it together with the next st on the needle.

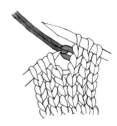

To resolve the gap on WS rows: Work to the turning point, slip the next st purlwise (the stitch past the turning point), pull on both ends of the CC yarn bringing up a loop. Insert LH needle into the loop from the bottom, slip the stitch on the RH needle back to the LH needle and purl it together with the loop.

Bias bind off

To work this kind of bind off, stop 1 st before end of row on the row preceding the bind off and turn work as instructed in the pattern. Slip 1 st purlwise from the LH to the RH needle, BO 1 st by bringing the unworked end st over the slipped st, then continue to BO sts normally. BO purlwise when binding off on a WS row.

Three-needle bind off

With RS together, hold the needles parallel. With a third needle, knit the first st of front and back needles together, *knit next st from each needle together (2 sts on RH needle), lift the first st over the second st and off the RH needle to BO 1 st; rep from * until all sts are bound off.

Backward loop cast on

Wrap yarn around left thumb from front to back and secure in palm with other fingers. Insert needle upwards through strand on thumb. Slip loop from thumb onto RH needle, pulling yarn to tighten. Rep from * for desired number of sts.

Chain (crochet)

Wrap the yarn around the crochet hook (yarn over) and draw it through the loop on the hook to form the first chain. Rep this step as many times as instructed. (The loop on the hook is never included when counting the number of chains.)

Abbreviations

k1-f/b (knit 1, front and back): Knit into the front loop of next st but leave that stitch on the needle, then knit into the back loop of same st. (1 st increased).

k1-r/b (knit 1 st in row below): To work this increase turn the LH needle slightly towards you so that the WS of the work can be seen. Insert RH needle form the top down into the purl stitch that sits below the first st on the LH needle. Knit this Stitch then knit the stitch on the needle.

k2tog: Knit 2 sts together (1 st decreased, leans to the right).

k3tog: Knit 3 sts together (2 st decreased, leans to the right).

M1R (make 1 right slanting): Insert LH needle from back to front under horizontal strand between st just worked and next st, knit lifted strand through the front loop (1 st increased).

M1L (make 1 left slanting): Insert LH needle from front to back under horizontal strand between st just worked and next st, knit lifted strand through the back loop (1 st increased).

p2tog: Purl 2 sts together (1 st decreased).

sk2p: Slip 1 st knitwise to RH needle, k2tog, pass slipped st over st created by k2tog (2 sts decreased, leans to the left).

ssk (slip, slip, knit): Slip 2 sts one at a time knitwise to the RH needle; return sts to LH needle in turned position and knit them together through the back loops (1 st decreased, leans to the left).

sssk (slip, slip, slip, knit): Slip 3 sts one at a time knitwise to the RH needle; return sts to LH needle in turned position and knit them together through the back loops (2 st decreased, leans to the left).

ssp (slip, slip, purl): Slip 2 sts one at a time knitwise to the RH needle; return sts to LH needle in turned position and purl them together through the back loops (1 st decreased).

w&t (wrap and turn): (RS) Slip the next st to the RH needle and bring the yarn to the front of work between the needles. Slip st back to the LH needle. Turn, and bring yarn to front between the needles, ready to work next row. To pick up wraps of RS work to wrapped st, insert the right needle into the wrap as if to knit (but do not lift it onto the left needle) and then into the st on the needle and knit together as one.

(WS) Slip the next st to the RH needle and bring the yarn to the back of the work between the needles. Slip st back to the LH needle. Turn and bring yarn to back between the needles, ready to work next row. To pick up wraps of WS work to wrapped st, pick up the wrap and place on left needle and purl it together with the next st on the needle

yo (yarn over): Bring yarn between needles to the front, then over RH needle ready to knit the next st (1 st increased).

yo (yarn over): Bring yarn between needles to the front, then over RH needle ready to knit the next st (1 st increased).

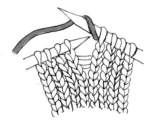

k1-r/b (knit 1 st in row below): To work this increase turn the LH needle slightly towards you so that the WS of the work can be seen. Insert RH needle form the top down into the purl stitch that sits below the first st on the LH needle. Knit this Stitch then knit the stitch on the needle.

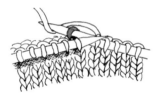

k2tog: Knit 2 sts together (1 st decreased, leans to the right).

k1-f/b : Knit into the front loop of next st but leave that stitch on the needle, then knit into the back loop of same st. (1 st increased).

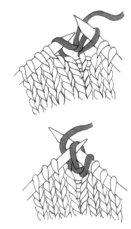

ssk (slip, slip, knit): Slip 2 sts one at a time knitwise to the RH needle; return sts to LH needle in turned position and knit them together through the back loops (1 st decreased, leans to the left).

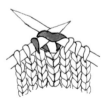

M1R (make 1 right slanting): Insert LH needle from back to front under horizontal strand between st just worked and next st, knit lifted strand through the front loop (1 st increased).

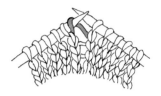

M1L (make 1 left slanting): Insert LH needle from front to back under horizontal strand between st just worked and next st, knit lifted strand through the back loop (1 st increased).

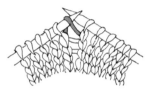

Picking up stitches
From a bound off or cast on edge:
Insert needle from front to back under one of the V shaped stitches that you can see along the top edge of the knitting (or the hole you can see at the top between two columns of stitches). Wrap working yarn around needle and draw a loop through to the other side to pick up 1 stitch.

From a vertical edge:
Insert needle from front to back at least one full stitch in from the edge of the knitting (this means you will be going under two strands of yarn). Wrap working yarn around needle and draw a loop through to the other side to pick up 1 stitch.

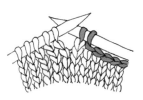

Binding off
Knit 2 stitches normally then *pass the first stitch worked over the next stitch to bind off 1 st. Knit one more stitch from the LH needle; rep from * until 1 stitch is left on the needle. Break yarn and draw through remaining stitch.

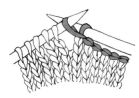

Standard Abbreviations

approx	approximately
beg	begin(ning); begin; begins
BO	bind off
BOR	beginning of round
CO	cast on
CC	contrasting color
circ	circular needle
cm	centimeter(s)
cont	continue(s); continuing
dec('d)	decrease(d)
dpn(s)	double-pointed needle(s)
est	establish(ed)
g	gram(s)
inc('d)	increase(d)
k	knit
LH	left hand
MC	main color
meas	measures
mm	millimeter(s)
m(s)	marker(s)
p	purl
patt(s)	pattern(s)
pc(s)	piece(s)
pm	place marker
psso	pass slipped stitch(es) over
rem	remain(ing)
rep	repeat; repeating
RH	right hand
rnd(s)	round(s)
RS	right side
sl	slip
sl m	slip marker
st(s)	stitch(es)
St st	stockinette stitch
tbl	through the back loop
tog	together
wyib	with yarn in back
wyif	with yarn in front
WS	wrong side
yd	yard(s)

bios

Gudrun Johnston originally hails from the Shetland Islands but now lives in Western Massachusetts. Her work often incorporates traditional Shetland techniques and motifs, featuring these timeless design elements in a contemporary context. She also loves to design using seamless construction methods and is always adding new techniques to her seamless knitting skills. See more of her designs at www.theshetlandtrader.com

Quince & Company was launched in 2010 by two knitwear designers and a mill owner who confess to a strong bias toward natural fibers and local manufacturing. Quince yarns are spun from American wool, or sourced from overseas suppliers who grow plants, raise animals, or make yarn in as earth- and labor-friendly a way as possible. Find out more at www.quinceandco.com

credits

styling Gudrun Johnston

photography& graphic design Carrie Bostick Hoge

models Jenn, Sedona, Cynthia, Izzy, Gudrun, and Maya

book printing Puritan Press

technical editor Jerusha Robinson

illustrations Maya Durham

knitters Nicole Dupuis and Margaux Hufnagel

To get your free ebook, please send an email to gudruncjohnston@gmail.com and use this code:
1112SHTRKWM